PRAISE FOR

WHAT WOULD JESUS ASK?

In this excellent new book, Dr. Jim Dixon raises deep, serious, life-changing questions in a way that reflects both scholarly intellect and the heart of a pastor. By turns, entertaining, encouraging and deeply convicting, *What Would Jesus Ask?* is a book people will be thinking and talking about for years to come. Whether read cover-to-cover in a single evening, or carefully parsed over weeks or months as a study guide, this is a great read!

WILLIAM L. ARMSTRONG
President, Colorado Christian University

This is a Jesus book about how to live life. It is probing, yet inspiring. Radical, but just what we need in our lives and in our world today! I invite you to read *What Would Jesus Ask*? and be transformed into a beautiful, powerful witness and follower of Jesus. Jim Dixon is a living example of what he writes.

ARTHUR BLESSITT
A pilgrim follower of Jesus, Luke 18:1

I love good questions because they have the power to transform us. In this book, Dr. Jim Dixon challenges readers with life's most important questions—the questions that Jesus would ask of us. His wisdom and insights will help you seek and find the fulfilling answers. I highly recommend this book.

MARK SANBORN
Acclaimed speaker and bestselling author of *The Fred Factor, Fred 2.0* and *You Don't Need a Title to Be a Leader*

Thinking back, it was a friend's challenging question that led me, at age 19, to reconsider how I was living and ultimately to commit my life to Christ. Later, another friend's question prompted me to study theology and apologetics. Not long after that, yet another friend's question was used to redirect me into full-time ministry.

Without a doubt, God has used questions from friends to shape, stretch and redirect me on my spiritual journey. Now, through this potent little book, you have the opportunity to let my pastor and friend, Dr. Jim Dixon, ask you some key questions. I believe God will use these questions to guide and grow you in your own journey of faith. So open up your heart—and these pages—to see what adventures God has in store for you!

MARK MITTELBERG
Bestselling author and co-director of The Institute at Cherry Hills

You hold in your hand ten of the most important questions in life. If you have not thought about them, you need to start now. But more importantly you hold in your hand answers that come from the Scriptures, and of course from Jesus Himself. Read and be enlighten.

ELMER L. TOWNS
Co founder, Liberty University, Lynchburg, Virginia

WHAT WOULD JESUS ASK

10 Questions That Will Transform Your Life

JIM DIXON

Regal

For more information and
special offers from Regal Books, email us at
subscribe@regalbooks.com

Published by Regal
From Gospel Light
Ventura, California, U.S.A.
www.regalbooks.com
Printed in the U.S.A.

Library of Congress Cataloging-in-Publication Data

Dixon, Jim, 1945-
What would Jesus ask? : 10 questions that will transform your life / Jim Dixon ; [foreword by] Lee Strobel.
pages cm
Summary: "What Would Jesus Do? or WWJD has become ubiquitous on T-shirts, coffee mugs, wristbands and church billboards. But when trying to define the Christian life Jesus intended His followers to live, a more valuable question is What Would Jesus Ask? Readers will find that, according to the Gospels, Jesus posed hundreds of questions that taken together lay a foundation for strong, vibrant and lasting faith. As individuals or groups wrestle with Jesus' questions, they will find the answers they need to live a more holistic and committed Christian life. Chapter Titles 1. Are You a Spiritual Person? 2. Do You Care About Others? 3. What Kind of Leader Are You? 4. What Will Be Your Legacy? 5. Do You Have Time for God? 6.When Will You Ever Have Enough? 7. Does Your Faith Influence Your Finances? 8. What Are You Afraid Of? 9. Will You Stand With Jesus? 10. What Does a Successful Life Look Like? "-- Provided by publisher.
Includes bibliographical references and index.
ISBN 978-0-8307-6740-3 (pbk.)
1. Christian life--Miscellanea. 2. Spirituality--Miscellanea. I. Title.
BV4501.3.D59 2013
248.4--dc23
2013011856

Rights for publishing this book outside the U.S.A. or in non-English languages are administered by Gospel Light Worldwide, an international not-for-profit ministry. For additional information, please visit www.glww.org, email info@glww.org, or write to Gospel Light Worldwide, 1957 Eastman Avenue, Ventura, CA 93003, U.S.A.

To order copies of this book and other Regal products in bulk quantities, please contact us at 1-800-446-7735.

CONTENTS

ACKNOWLEDGMENTS

The following people have provided the necessary reminders, urgings, gifts and talents to get this book completed. Thank you all!

Steve Rabey—for using your considerable editing and writing skills and for partnering with me. Your love for Christ and your knowledge of truth are inspiring.

Jim Shaffer and Blythe Daniel—for faithful leadership in the publishing process. Thank you, Jim and Blythe.

Lee Strobel—for your friendship and for writing the foreword to this book. Thank you for your graciousness to me and for your great service to the kingdom of Christ.

Dutch Franz—for encouraging me to write books and for partnering with me in ministry.

Barbara Dixon—you are awesome! Thank you for being my partner in life and ministry.

Cherry Hills Community Church staff, elders and congregation—I am humbled and grateful to be your pastor and friend.

FOREWORD

Jim Dixon is a rare combination. He's a scholar with an incisive mind and the ability to communicate complex issues clearly. He's a pastor with an unusually tender heart. He's a leader who is first and foremost a follower of Christ. He's attuned to popular culture, but he's grounded in eternal truths. He thinks profoundly, laughs heartily and cares deeply.

Whether he's with his family, his friends or members of the congregation he has led for more than 30 years, Jim is consistently marked by an authentic love for those around him. In fact, he wrote this book because he cares so much about people that he doesn't want them to miss God's ultimate purpose and meaning for their lives.

Just as Jesus used questions to penetrate our pretenses, expose our motivations and nudge us in the right direction, so too Jim uses this book to explore a series of provocative and life-changing questions to help us move closer to God. As we wrestle with these very real—and vitally important—issues, we will find ourselves growing spiritually in fresh and exciting ways.

For me, the most transformative teaching isn't always the material that expands my mind. As important as information is, I find that real maturity comes when I'm encouraged to apply God's teaching to my life in everyday, practical ways. That's what Jim will help you do in this unique and powerful book. Let him guide you through a series of questions with a ready mind and an open heart, and you will walk away a changed person—for the better.

I've become a more devoted follower of Jesus having spent several years under Jim's preaching. Now, you will have the opportunity to let him take you on a journey of personal and spiritual development. In the end, you'll see why I value Jim so much as a friend, a leader and a godly model.

Lee Strobel
Author, *The Case for Christ* and *The Case for Faith*

1

An Invitation to Wrestle with Life's Big Questions

Every day, each one of us answers thousands of questions without even realizing it. *What will I wear today? What do I want for lunch? Do I really need that new smart phone with its expensive data plan? And what will I do tonight: watch a movie or catch up on my reading?* Most of these questions are so simple that we aren't even aware we are answering them.

Meanwhile, there are more complex questions that seem to bubble up from deep within. *Who am I? What is my purpose in life? How can I experience happiness and live with a sense of meaning?*

Philosophers and religious teachers have been challenging people to wrestle with these kinds of *big questions* for thousands of years. That includes the teacher who repeatedly asked His followers questions like these:

- Why do you call me 'Lord, Lord' and not do what I command?
- Where is your faith?
- Why are you anxious about clothes?
- Why do you notice the splinter in your brother's eye yet fail to perceive the wooden beam in your own eye?
- But who do you say that I am?
- Why does this generation seek a sign?
- Do you not yet understand or comprehend? Are your hearts hardened? Do you have eyes and still not see? Ears and not hear?
- Do you love me?

If these questions sound familiar to you, that's because they are some of the 100-plus questions asked by Jesus during His three years of public ministry. People think of Jesus primarily as a teacher and a preacher, and I believe He was the greatest teacher who ever lived. But He did more than merely spell out answers to life's mysteries; He also raised unsettling questions that forced His listeners to drill down and probe the deeper things of life.

That's precisely why Jesus regularly asked such complex and even mystifying questions, challenging His disciples and the others who followed Him to stop, think and consider the life-changing lessons He was teaching them. As a great teacher, He knew that students learn better when they are challenged and provoked. Interrogation often works better than oration. He also knew that good questions go beyond simple multiple-choice items that appear on many classroom quizzes. Complex questions about life's big issues challenge us to dive more deeply into the truth.

That's why I am writing this book. Every week millions of people hear sermons or homilies designed to provide answers and guidance for life's challenges. I've preached well over a thousand sermons myself. In this book, I want to do more than preach to you. I want to ask you a series of questions about your heart, your passions, your core values, your goals in life, and the way you spend your time and your money. I hope that by asking these questions I can encourage you to give more time and energy to reflecting on the questions that are more important than what you will eat for lunch or what you will watch on TV tonight. I pray that you may think more deeply about the life you are now living and the kind of life you want to live in the future.

From Platitudes to Attitudes

Every school student knows there are some classes we take only because they are required, and for some of us, our main goal in these required classes is to survive well enough to get a passing grade. We study course materials only long enough to pass a test, but then we later forget everything we "learned."

Then there are other classes that challenge us to fully invest our time and energies in doing the readings and course work. Perhaps the subject of a particular class clicks with us and brings out our innate curiosity and passion. Or maybe we have a good teacher who helps us see how the lessons in the textbook relate to important issues in the larger world around us.

The subject we're going to explore in this book can be called "Life 101." My goal is to help you see that living the Christian life requires more of you and me than merely gathering together a smattering of religious information in our already overstuffed brains. Instead, I believe that life is a never-ending process of learning and growing that continually challenges us to reconsider how we live and what we value.

Ultimately, following Christ can lead to complete life transformation; but transformation only happens if you commit yourself to *wrestling* with what Jesus is trying to teach you and *incorporating* these life lessons into your heart. The result of this life-long growth process is spiritual maturity.

The New Testament tells us that some people are spiritual babies who survive on a diet of milk, while others are spiritually mature people who eat meat (see 1 Cor. 3:2; Heb. 5:12). I don't want you to remain a babe. I want you to grow into maturity, and that comes from accepting Christ's challenge to reconsider the beliefs and attitudes that form our attitudes about life.

What is it that makes one person a spiritual infant while another is spiritually mature? I believe the answer can be summed up by the terms *knowing* and *doing.* We may memorize every verse of the Bible, but if this knowledge does not change us on the inside or transform our behavior on the outside, we are merely hearers of God's Word, not doers.

James tells us, "For if any one is a hearer of the word and not a doer, he is like a man who observes his natural face in a mirror; for he observes himself and goes away and at once forgets what he was like. But he who looks into the perfect law, the law of liberty, and perseveres, being no hearer that forgets but a doer that acts, he shall be blessed in his doing" (Jas. 1:23-25).

Information about God or the Bible does not make a person a Christian. Only life transformation demonstrates that one is a follower of Christ. The person who desires to grow closer to God is focused on attitudes, not platitudes. In other words, you need to do more than *know* in your mind that God wants us to love our neighbors. You need to allow God to transform your heart so that you actually do love them. This requires a willingness to go beneath the surface and wrestle with the many profound questions Jesus asks us.

As a pastor, I know members of my congregation who say they believe in something with all their hearts, but then they don't always connect the dots between their beliefs, their attitudes and their behaviors. In this book I want to help you connect the dots by asking you 10 of the toughest questions Jesus asks us.

I'm not going to ask you to send me your answers so that I can give you a letter grade. Instead, your success will be judged by the number of times you scratch your head or say *hmm* to yourself as you think about these all-important life questions.

Are you ready to begin?

Reflection Questions

1. How do you tend to respond when someone asks you a question?

    - Provide a thoughtful response
    - Respond without thinking through the question
    - Ignore or redirect the question
    - Pause, ponder, and reflect upon the question

2. What do you think this says about your unique personality?

3. Why do you think Jesus asked so many questions of people? What was the meaning behind such a teaching strategy?

4. How can you make sure you are an actual doer of God's words and not merely a hearer of such instruction (see Jas. 1:22-25)?

5. As you begin to read this book and consider some of the big questions of life, take a moment and ask God to give you an open and receptive heart to hear and respond as He would desire. Will you commit to sharing or journaling your response to Him so that you can implant this in your mind as you continue to move toward Him?

2

Are You a Spiritual Person?

There are two ways through life: the way of nature and the way of grace. You have to choose which one you will follow. This insight didn't come from a sermon or a book on theology, but from *Tree of Life*, one of the most unusual and powerful movies of recent years. Starring Brad Pitt as a conflicted man trying desperately to balance the competing demands of work, creativity, marriage and parenting, *Tree of Life* is a *spiritual* movie. By that I mean it does more than entertain us and dazzle our senses. This film tries to touch us on a deeper level and challenge us about what we think and how we live.

It's one thing to talk about spiritual movies or books or songs, but what about people? Some people seem sensitive to God's grace and exhibit this grace in their lives, while others seem consumed with the natural side of life: food, money, possessions and status.

Which kind of person are you? Do you live according to *nature* or *grace*? Jesus asked an important question: "For what does it profit a man, to gain the whole world and forfeit his life?" (Mark 8:36). As the pastor of a big church in one of the wealthiest counties in the United States, I regularly ask people similar questions. It's clear that we live in a world that is both physical and spiritual, but which is your priority?

You may call yourself a Christian, go to church regularly and live according to Christian principles, but is your soul—the inner spiritual part of yourself—alive and growing? The best way to tell whether or not you are a spiritual person is to compare your life to the three characteristics of the lives of spiritual people found in the Bible. Let's take a look at these characteristics to see how you measure up.

Characteristic #1 of Spiritual People: New Life

When Dr. Frankenstein assembled his monster from body parts he had harvested from various corpses, he still needed one more thing to complete his creation: the spark of life, which was provided by a handy thunderbolt.

The same goes for us. Are we just a collection of bones, muscles, tissues and organs, or are we spiritual people? The Bible teaches that a spiritual person is a person who has experienced regeneration and rebirth. This concept of new life is explored in John's Gospel, which records an interesting meeting between Jesus and a man named Nicodemus.

Nicodemus was a member of the Pharisees, a devout group of Jews who lived at the time of Jesus. Even more impressive, Nicodemus was a member of the Sanhedrin, a panel of judges that was appointed in every city in Jewish lands. This meant his fellow Jews viewed him as a very religious person.

But things aren't always the way they seem on the surface. While some people saw Nicodemus as a spiritual person, Jesus said there was one important thing missing: "Truly, truly, I say to you, unless one is born anew, he cannot see the kingdom of God."

These words confused Nicodemus, so he asked Jesus, "How can a man be born when he is old? Can he enter a second time into his mother's womb and be born?"

Jesus answered, "Truly, truly, I say to you, unless one is born of water and the Spirit, he cannot enter the kingdom of God. That which is born of the flesh is flesh, and that which is born of the Spirit is spirit" (John 3:5-6).

As we read the New Testament and see how Jesus interacted with people, He often went beyond their outward appearance to assess the state of their souls. When Jesus looked into the soul of Nicodemus, He could see that his soul had not experienced spiritual rebirth.

The Bible makes it clear that you are born again when you accept Jesus for who the Bible says He is (God's only Son), accept Him into your heart and soul as your Savior (who will redeem you from your sins), obey Him as Lord of your life (follow His teachings and His example), and make a commitment to follow Him and become more like Him every day. This may sound complicated, but it doesn't need to be.

Every year, our church hosts a big Easter service for thousands of people at Fiddler's Green. (It was formerly known by a corporate-sponsored name: Comfort Dental Amphitheater!) Members of our church sometimes ask why we pack up and leave our nice, comfortable church, with its cushioned seating, good lighting and professional acoustics, for this outdoor park. The answer comes from people like the young man who came up to me one day and said, "I just want you to know that six years ago at Fiddler's Green, I asked Jesus into my heart."

Being a spiritual person doesn't happen by adopting a philosophy of life, joining an organization or being good—even though these are all good things. Being a spiritual person begins with experiencing new life. And that's just the first step of a life-long process, as the apostle Peter explained:

> You have been born anew, not of perishable seed but of imperishable, through the living and abiding word of God; for "All flesh is like grass and all its glory like the flower of grass. The grass withers, and the flower falls, but the word of the Lord abides for ever." That word is the good news which was preached to you. . . . So put away all malice and all guile and insincerity and envy and all slander. Like newborn babes, long for the pure

> spiritual milk, that by it you may grow up to salvation; for you have tasted the kindness of the Lord (1 Pet. 1:23-25; 2:1-3).

Have you been born anew? If so, you have stepped out on the journey toward being a spiritual person. If not, you need to put this book down right now and ask Jesus into your heart, just like the young man did at our Easter service, and just like I did as a young child. If you don't know how to do that, seek out a trusted Christian friend or a pastor who can help you.

The rest of this book can help you after you've taken this first step, but there's no other way to begin; as Jesus told Nicodemus, "That which is born of the flesh is flesh, and that which is born of the Spirit is spirit."

Characteristic #2 of Spiritual People: Being Like Jesus

It's okay to behave like a newborn babe for a while, but then it's time to grow up. It's the same for the spiritual life. Being born again is merely the first step of a lifelong journey toward spiritual maturity.

The best way to make progress on this journey is to become more like Jesus every day. No matter what your life was like before, now you need to walk in the footsteps of Jesus if you are going to be a spiritual person.

The apostle Paul tells us what being like Jesus requires: "Forgetting what lies behind and straining forward to what lies ahead, I press on toward the goal for the prize of the upward call of God in Christ Jesus" (Phil. 3:13-14).

The goal of a spiritual person is to be like Christ by experiencing what Paul calls the fullness of Christ (see Eph. 1:23; 3:19). But often, many of us are so full of ourselves that we don't experience the fullness of Christ, as I know all too well from my own life.

Paul was one of the greatest Christian teachers who ever lived, but the person who teaches me more than anyone else about how to be more like Jesus is my longsuffering wife, Barb.

It seems that every three or four days Barb and I have a conflict or disagreement that shows how childish I can be. Nearly every time we have an argument, I engage in some of my usual immature behaviors, like being defensive, denying the reality of what she is saying, insisting on having my own way, or simply getting angry and walking away.

Later on, I have had some time to cool down and think about what Barb has been saying to me. At that point, I can see things more clearly. I can see that she loves me and cares for me, and that she wants the best for me in life. That's when I seek her out, apologize for my childish behavior and try to make things right.

Experiences like this explain why the Protestant Reformer Martin Luther called marriage a "school for character." The intimate relationship we can have with our spouse gives us great opportunities to learn to be more Christlike, but only if we are willing to grow and allow God to make us more like His Son. I have learned much from Barb about how God's grace can transform my inner character flaws and calm my anger.

What about you? Perhaps you find yourself getting angry with your partner or your close friends. Or does your anger reveal itself in episodes of road rage? Sometimes the nicest people can become little monsters behind the wheel. Or does your dark side come out when you're at a sporting event and an official makes a foul call that you don't agree with? Basketball and football games can also be schools for character, particularly when your child or grandchild is playing.

In fact, every moment of life is an opportunity to grow if you truly desire to become more like Jesus. That's especially true for people like me who have so much to learn. Are you seeking to be like Jesus with all your heart and soul, or are you more concerned about other priorities? If you really want to be a spiritual person, you'll move "pursuing Christlikeness" closer to the top of your to-do list.

Characteristic #3 of Spiritual People: Ongoing Spiritual Growth

If you've experienced spiritual rebirth and you're passionate about being more like Jesus, the third characteristic you will need to be a spiritual person is growth. This doesn't mean you will ever arrive at a state of sinless perfection during your life. But it does mean that if you are truly a spiritual person, your spirituality will reveal itself in ongoing spiritual growth.

That's because being spiritual is all about inner transformation. Transformation begins when you are born again, but it is never totally completed in this life. Paul describes the kind transformation Christ desires to see in us: "And we all, with unveiled face, beholding the glory of the Lord, are being changed into his likeness from one degree of glory to another; for this comes from the Lord who is the Spirit" (2 Cor. 3:18).

Anything that is truly alive must grow, including your soul. If you're committed to taking this journey of spiritual growth, I want to let you know about the three essential ingredients you will need along the way.

1. Soul Food

Jesus miraculously transformed a few fish and a few loaves of bread into enough food to feed thousands of people (see Matt. 14:13-21; Mark 6:31-44; Luke 9:10-17; John 6:5-15), but His main concern was food for the soul:

> "Do not labor for the food which perishes, but for the food which endures to eternal life, which the Son of man will give to you; for on him has God the Father set his seal." Then they said to him, "What must we do, to be doing the works of God?" Jesus answered them, "This is the work of God, that you believe in him whom he has sent. . . . I am the bread of life; he who comes to me shall not hunger, and he who believes in me shall never thirst" (John 6:27-29,35).

Jesus is looking for followers who hunger for spiritual food as regularly as their bodies hunger for physical nourishment: "It is written: 'Man shall not live by bread alone, but by every word that proceeds from the mouth of God'" (Matt. 4:4).

People who seek spiritual nourishment feast on the Bible, the Word of God. Some people do this in the morning, grabbing a cup of coffee and then heading to a comfortable chair for a quick meal of soul food before beginning the day's tasks. Others save their feasting for the nighttime, allowing the nourishment to feed their rest and their dreams. Others take a break during the workday to head outside or to a quiet space for a time of reading and meditating on God's Word.

During my times of daily Bible reading and reflection, I focus on different portions of Scripture. I turn to the Gospels (Matthew, Mark, Luke and John) to learn more about Jesus so that I can become more like Him every day. I read from the book of Psalms before my times of prayer, because many of the psalms themselves are prayers to God. I regularly read a few proverbs from the book of Proverbs, which provide nourishing nuggets of wisdom. And I read the book of Acts and the various New Testament letters (Romans through Jude) to see how the earliest Christians applied their faith to the challenges of daily life.

I know some people who try to read the entire Bible from beginning to end every year, which is something you can do yourself if you read between three and four chapters every day. I know others who read a few chapters from the Old Testament and a few chapters from the New Testament each day. Others focus on one book at a time, using commentaries or other resources to help them dig deeper into one important portion of the Bible.

There are many different ways that you can get the soul food you need from God's Word. The point is to follow the advice Peter gave us earlier in this chapter concerning proper spiritual nutrition: "Like newborn babes, long for the pure spiritual milk, that by it you may grow up to salvation" (1 Pet. 2:2).

2. Soul Training

Americans are getting bigger and less healthy. A third or more of us are overweight. For many, these problems are caused by exercising less and eating more. I'm here to tell you that souls can grow flabby, too, if they're not properly trained, and the best form of soul training is through service and ministry to others in Jesus' name.

What better way to further the inward transformation that is taking place in your soul than by being Jesus' hands and feet, reaching out to people in need, whether their needs be physical or spiritual.

I emphasize putting faith into action through soul training because Christianity is about more than just head knowledge; it's also about stepping out and making the world a better place. Being a spiritual person is about more than "me, me, me." It's also about "you, you, you" and your needs and issues.

Here at Cherry Hills Community Church, nearly half of our more than 4,500 members are involved in regular service and ministry. More than a thousand people serve the church every week as we gather together in worship and learning. Some serve as elders; others teach Sunday School or sing in the choir. During the week, hundreds more serve as small-group leaders. Others roll up their sleeves and serve the community, whether at local food banks for the hungry, urban ministries to disadvantaged youth, after-school tutoring sessions for struggling students, or by providing protection for battered women.

I'm not telling you about this to brag about what a great church we have (though we do!). I'm trying to demonstrate our belief that soul training is not something we merely think about or talk about—it's something we *do*!

Just as bodily training promotes physical health and strength, so too soul training grows the soul. As Paul told Timothy, a brother who helped Paul carry the burdens of ministry, "Train yourself in godliness; for while bodily training is of some value, godliness is of value in every way, as it holds promise for the present life and also for the life to come" (1 Tim. 4:7-8).

People who are physically flabby and out of shape will never be able to run a marathon race up one of Colorado's 54 "fourteeners" (the 54 mountain peaks that exceed 14,000 feet in elevation). Likewise, the spiritual life is not a walk in the park. It's a challenging, lifelong journey that requires soul training. If you fail to train your soul, then your progress as a spiritual person will be bogged down by spiritual flabbiness. That's why you need to exercise your soul through reaching out and serving others in Jesus' name.

3. Soul Partners

Earlier in this chapter I told you about my wife, Barb, and how she has lovingly helped me learn what it means to be a follower of Christ. Likewise, you need soul partners in your life if you want to grow toward spiritual maturity.

If you are fortunate like I am, your spouse is a valuable soul partner. But Barb, even as amazing as she is, cannot be the only one I depend on to help me become a more spiritual person. I need men in my life with whom I can share honestly about my struggles as a man. I also need my brothers and sisters in the church to help me, love me, pray for me and care for me when I am in need. Likewise, they need the same kind of love and support from me.

Every one of us will find different soul partners along the way, but the point is that Christianity is not a solo performance. We need each other in order to grow. We need soul partners who encourage us in Christ, laugh and cry with us, exhort us and—when necessary—rebuke us. We need soul partners with whom we can be vulnerable, confess our sins and seek accountability as we take the long journey toward spiritual maturity.

The apostle John tells us how our soul partners can help us walk in the light of God's love: "If we say we have fellowship with him while we walk in darkness, we lie and do not live according to the truth; but if we walk in the light, as he is in the light, we have fellowship with one another, and the blood of Jesus his Son cleanses us from all sin" (1 John 1:6-7).

It's really pretty simple. Spiritual people have experienced spiritual rebirth; their main goal in life is to be more like Jesus; and they put their faith into action by studying God's Word, reaching out in service to others and walking side by side with fellow travelers on the journey of spiritual growth.

If you truly want to be a spiritual person, this is the map you must follow to find your way safely home.

Reflection Questions

1. Read 1 Corinthians 2:14–3:3. In this passage, Paul describes three kinds of people: (1) natural, (2) spiritual, and (3) carnal (fleshly). As you ponder these descriptions, which one best describes you today? Deep down, which kind of person do you really want to be?

2. Becoming a spiritual person begins with experiencing a new or spiritual birth that brings you into a relationship with Christ. (If this is something you desire for your life, please see the postscript for instructions on how to initiate and experience this kind of relationship.) What are one or two practices that would help you conduct your life each day in a manner that is more consistent with the heart and character of Christ?

3. Do you have any kind of regular Bible reading plan or practice? If not, what will you do to incorporate the teachings of Scripture into your life?

4. What is one area you could pursue to use your gifts and talents in serving Christ?

5. Do you have a group of people with whom you meet regularly to encourage each other toward growth and maturity as spiritual people? If not, how will you find a small group of believers in Christ to go through life's journey?

3

Do You Care About Others?

Dorothea Dix was born in Maine, in 1802, and by the time she died in 1887, she had changed the world. Thank God her doctor was wrong about her dying young.

Dorothea was 29 years old and working as a schoolteacher when her doctor gave her some bad news. She had a rare lung disease and didn't have long to live. After hearing the news, she quit her teaching job and went on vacation to England, where someone gave her a Bible. She read the New Testament, then went back and read it again, over and over. As she read, the words on the page came to life in her soul. She encountered the resurrected Jesus Christ and gave her life to Him. Then she asked Christ an important question:

"Lord, what do You want me to do?"

In her soul, she heard the Lord say, "I want you to care."

"What do You mean, Lord? Care about whom? Care about what?"

The Lord said, "I want you to care about the least."

Some people might have been confused about what this meant, but Dorothea had read the New Testament so many times that she quickly remembered this powerful passage from Matthew 25 about the sheep and the goats:

> When the Son of man comes in his glory, and all the angels with him, then he will sit on his glorious throne. Before him will be gathered all the nations, and he will separate them one from another as a shepherd separates the sheep from the goats, and he will place the sheep at his right hand, but the goats at the left.
>
> Then the King will say to those at his right hand, "Come, O blessed of my Father, inherit the kingdom prepared for you from the foundation of the world; for I was hungry and you gave me food, I was thirsty and you gave me drink, I was a stranger and you welcomed me, I was naked and you clothed me, I was sick and you visited me, I was in prison and you came to me."
>
> Then the righteous will answer him, "Lord, when did we see thee hungry and feed thee, or thirsty and give thee drink? And when did we see thee a stranger and welcome thee, or naked and clothe thee? And when did we see thee sick or in prison and visit thee?"

> And the King will answer them, "Truly, I say to you, as you did it to one of the least of these my brethren, you did it to me."
>
> Then he will say to those at his left hand, "Depart from me, you cursed, into the eternal fire prepared for the devil and his angels; for I was hungry and you gave me no food, I was thirsty and you gave me no drink, I was a stranger and you did not welcome me, naked and you did not clothe me, sick and in prison and you did not visit me."
>
> Then they also will answer, "Lord, when did we see thee hungry or thirsty or a stranger naked or sick or in prison, and did not minister to thee?"
>
> Then he will answer them, "Truly, I say to you, as you did it not to one of the least of these, you did it not to me." And they will go away into eternal punishment, but the righteous into eternal life (Matt. 25:31-46).

Wanting to get to work on her new assignment from Jesus, Dorothea returned to the U.S. right away and started a Bible study for prisoners at a Boston penitentiary. While there, she saw that the prison conditions were inhumane. The prison was overcrowded, poorly heated and unsanitary. People were being whipped, and they were being starved to death and treated in a subhuman fashion.

I know there were some Christians then (and now) who might say, "These people are prisoners and lawbreakers. They deserve everything they get." Not Dorothea. She worked to improve the conditions at the Boston prison, and when that task was accomplished, she singlehandedly launched a prison reform movement that took off throughout America.

That's not all. While working at the prison in Boston, Dorothea witnessed that mentally disabled people were being thrown into prison and forced to live alongside convicted murderers and prostitutes. Jesus hadn't specifically mentioned the mentally ill in Matthew 25, but Dorothea felt they fit the definition of "the least," so she began working on their behalf, as well, changing the way these people were treated, not only in prisons but in many areas of life.

Still, that's not all this woman did. Successful with many of her efforts in America, she felt a calling to help the least in other nations. Even though she remained weak and in poor health, she traveled to England, Scotland, France, Austria, Italy, Greece, Turkey, Russia, Sweden, Denmark, Holland, Belgium and Germany to promote prison reform and care for the mentally disabled in those nations. When she returned to America, she was appointed Superintendent of the United States Army Nursing Corps during the Civil War.

Today, few people have heard of Dorothea Dix, in part because she insisted on anonymity, and prohibited organizations from naming hospitals and treatment centers after her. When she finally died at the age of 85, President Grover Cleveland hailed her as the greatest woman America had ever produced.

I wonder what Dorothea Dix would have done with her life if her doctor had not told her that she would die young. More importantly, I wonder about you. Have you ever asked Jesus this simple question: *Lord, what do You want me to do?* The answer to this question may be found in the passage about the sheep and the goats. Do you want to be a sheep? If so, are you willing to care for the least?

Resurrecting the Incarnation

I love Christian holidays, particularly Easter, which celebrates the resurrection of Christ; and I love Christmas, which celebrates Jesus' incarnation into human form and birth to His mother, the Virgin Mary. Unfortunately, most of us forget all about this concept of incarnation as soon as we pack up our Christmas decorations.

That's too bad, because in order to be the sheep Jesus wants us to be, we need to do what Jesus did. That doesn't mean we need to be born to a virgin, but it does mean we need to incarnate ourselves into the lives of other people who need a caring hand. Jesus wants us to be His sheep. He wants us to move beyond our personal comfort zone so that we may incarnate ourselves in the world of the least, enabling Jesus to touch these needy souls through us.

Goats may be saved, and they may love God, but that love has not transformed them so profoundly that they desire to care for the least. Sheep, on the other hand, are willing to be incarnational. Through their experience of the love and grace of God, sheep care deeply about others, particularly the least, who are hungry, thirsty, naked and imprisoned.

Incarnation has been a complex and controversial theological topic. In church history there have been six great ecclesiastical councils—or general councils—where church leaders deliberated on the precise meaning of key Christian teachings.

Incarnation was a hot topic at the first ecclesiastical council at Nicaea, summoned by Constantine the Great, the Roman Emperor, in the year 325. Here, the greatest theologians and the most powerful church leaders of the day debated topics such as, What does incarnation really mean? What does it mean to say that Jesus was God in the flesh? What does it mean to say He was the "God man," fully divine and fully human? Their decisions laid the foundation for Christian theology down to our own time.

As important as these debates were, practically speaking, they missed the point. They didn't discuss how love was the motivation behind the Incarnation, as we see in John 3:16: "God so loved the world that he gave his only Son, that whoever believes in him should not perish but have eternal life."

Paul beautifully describes this kind of incarnational love in his letter to the Philippians:

> So if there is any encouragement in Christ, any incentive of love, any participation in the Spirit, any affection and sympathy, complete my joy by being of the same mind, having the same love, being in full accord and of one mind.
>
> Do nothing from selfishness or conceit, but in humility count others better than yourselves. Let each of you look not only to his own interests, but also to the interests of others.

> Have this mind among yourselves, which is yours in Christ Jesus, who, though he was in the form of God, did not count equality with God a thing to be grasped, but emptied himself, taking the form of a servant, being born in the likeness of men. And being found in human form he humbled himself and became obedient unto death, even death on a cross.
>
> Therefore God has highly exalted him and bestowed on him the name which is above every name, that at the name of Jesus every knee should bow, in heaven and on earth and under the earth, and every tongue confess that Jesus Christ is Lord, to the glory of God the Father (Phil. 2:1-11).

Jesus was a servant who emptied Himself in the service of others, and He wants us to do the same. If we don't, we are goats.

So why don't more Christians today love the least? Part of the reason is that we don't even *like* the least. We feel they are different from us, and we would rather love people who are like us, and who love us back.

Loving the Least

One of the main reasons some of the Christians I know fail to reach out to the least is because they want to spend their time around "winners" so that they can be a winner, too. We don't want to empty ourselves in the service of people we consider losers, because we don't see what's in it for us. Instead of reaching out to the people Jesus wants us to care for, we isolate and protect ourselves from them, building barriers that prevent us from having any contact.

In addition to not liking the least, there's another problem. We see people who are different from us in their lifestyle or their politics as bad people. If we support one political party, we disdain people who support another party. We don't merely disagree with them; we brand them as less patriotic or less human than we are. We dislike them and avoid them.

Timothy Keller, pastor of Redeemer Presbyterian Church in New York City, described this issue in his book *Counterfeit Gods.* Keller shows how our political idolatry causes us to be less Christlike to people who disagree with us:

> So many people now respond to U.S. political trends in such an extreme way. When either party wins an election, a certain percentage of the losing side talks openly about leaving the country. They become agitated and fearful for the future. They have put the kind of hope in their political leaders and policies that once was reserved for God and the work of the gospel. . . . Opponents are not considered to be simply mistaken, but to be evil. After the last presidential election, my 84 year old mother observed, "It used to be that whoever was elected as your president, even if he wasn't the one you voted for, he was still your president. That doesn't seem to be the case any longer." After each election, there is now a significant number of people who see

> the incoming president lacking moral legitimacy. The increasing political polarization and bitterness we see in U.S. politics today is a sign that we have made political activism into a form of religion. . . . [We] identify something besides sin as the main problem with the world and something besides God as the main remedy. That demonizes something that is not completely bad, and makes an idol out of something that cannot be the ultimate good.[1]

Most churches in America are racially and socially homogenous. That means we choose to be around people that are like us politically, racially, economically and socially. Why do we allow these differences to keep us separate?

Jesus tells us that at the final judgment there will be only two groups of people. There will be the sheep and there will be the goats. Jesus will separate these two kinds of people into their respective groups. The sheep will be placed at His right hand and welcomed into the Kingdom prepared for them since before the foundation of the world. The goats, meanwhile, will be placed at Jesus' left, where they will be consigned to eternal punishment.

You and I may look around the world and make our own judgments about the kinds of groupings that make sense to us: liberal or conservative; poor or rich; white or black. But when we divide up the world this way, our vision contradicts the vision of Jesus. We see things the way we want to see them, not the way He wants.

We make things very complicated and get very worked up and anxious about the diversity we see around us. But for Jesus, everything is simple. He wants us to be sheep. He wants us to be those who care about people, particularly about people who are hurting. The sheep give food and drink to the hungry and thirsty. They welcome the stranger. They clothe the naked. They visit the sick and those in prison. When the sheep show this kind of love to hurting men and women, they also show this same love to Jesus in mysterious and miraculous ways.

Many Ways to Love the Least

Earlier, we saw how Dorothea Dix loved "the least of these" by reaching out to prisoners and the mentally disabled. Now I want to introduce you to two more of Jesus' sheep.

In 1920, Lewis Lawes began a new job as warden of Sing Sing Correctional Facility in New York, which was also known as the "old hellhole." Lawes transformed the prison through a variety of reform efforts and new programs that included educational activities, sports teams and more humane discipline. But when praised for his work, this devoted Christian demurred, saying, "I didn't do it. My wife did it."

Kathryn Lawes was a devoted wife and mother of three children. She loved her family, and she loved her Lord. One would expect that she would stay clear of her husband's workplace. Instead, she did what she could to show her incarnational love for the prisoners.

She did one particular thing that was beautiful and powerful. Whenever the prisoners would have a basketball game, she would go, taking her three children with her. There they would sit in the stands and cheer on the players from both teams when they played well.

Early on, some of the prisoners would ask, "Who's that in the stands?"

"That's the warden's wife and her children," said the other prisoners. And in time, the men counted on seeing Kathryn and the kids at their games.

That's not all she did. When she learned that some of the prisoners at Sing Sing were blind, she learned Braille so that she could help them learn how to read again. When she learned that some of the prisoners at Sing Sing were deaf, she learned sign language so that she could communicate with them.

Sadly, Kathryn Lawes died after a fall in 1937. When news of her death reached Sing Sing, hardened criminals and longtime convicts wept openly. On the day of her funeral, 200 of the prisoners were allowed to attend the ceremony under strict supervision. Some even asked permission to stand and share their memories of her. As the prisoners' eulogies continued, many of the men said the same thing: "Kathryn Lawes was Jesus Christ in the flesh to us."[2]

What about you?

Do you really care about others?

Are you Jesus in the flesh to somebody in need?

Do you incarnate yourself into the world of others to share the love and mercy of Jesus in their midst?

Do you care for the least? Do you feed the hungry, clothe the naked and visit those who are in prison?

And when Jesus passes His final judgment, will you be found among the sheep or the goats?

REFLECTION QUESTIONS

1. What is stirring in your heart after reading this chapter?

2. How do you tend to view people who . . .

   - Are different from you?
   - Are not of the same social/economic class as you?
   - Who hold different political views?
   - Who don't share the same moral values as you?
   - Who are deemed the outcasts of our culture?

3. Read Colossians 3:12-14. How can you begin to exhibit the caring heart that Paul describes in these verses?

4. What would help you to begin to view all people through the eyes of Jesus? What difference do you think this would make in your life?

Consider trying this experiment. For the next 30 days, do one act of caring and kindness each day on behalf of another person: a family member, a friend, a co-worker or a total stranger. At the end of the 30 days, pause and consider how that practice influenced your life. Commit to do some research and find a place where you could serve a person or group of people who would be in the category of "the least of these."

Notes

1. Timothy Keller, *Counterfeit Gods: The Empty Promises of Money, Sex, and Power, and the Only Hope that Matters* (New York: Dutton, 2009).
2. "Convicts Mourn Wife of Warden," Pittsburgh Post-Gazette, November 2, 1937. http://news.google.com/

4

What Is Your #1 Goal as a Parent?

As a parent, what is the most important thing you can do for your child? Some parents say the most important thing is providing for a good education, which can lead to a better career and higher lifetime earnings.

Some parents focus on sports, health and physical fitness. If kids eat right, get plenty of exercise and supervised competition, and practice good dental hygiene, they will be healthier and happier for a long and positive life.

Some people are trying out Asian models of parenting that sometimes seem strict, or even harsh, when compared to Western approaches. The bestselling book *The Battle Hymn of the Tiger Mother* introduced readers to a tough-love parenting model, with the emphasis on "tough." Author Amy Chua described a Chinese approach that favors tossing kids out into the cold if they don't listen or obey, and insists that kids spend long hours every day practicing piano.

Some parents try jump-starting the process of raising a child before that child is even born, using the latest medical technology to influence their future child's hair color or tooth structure in the womb.

Then there are those who seem to fit the description of "helicopter parents." These parents hover over their children just like a helicopter hovers over the ground. I loved this description from a *Time* magazine article:

> We just wanted what was best for our kids. We bought macrobiotic cupcakes and hypoallergenic socks, hired tutors to correct a 5-year-old's "pencil-holding deficiency," hooked up broadband connections in the tree house but took down the swing set after the second skinned knee. We hovered over every school, playground and practice field.[1]

Parenting is difficult. Raising a child is one of the most awesome and most daunting challenges we face in life. It's no wonder people who are anxious about doing it just right have developed so many competing approaches.

That's why I titled this chapter with a question: "What Is Your #1 Goal as a Parent?" There are many different ways to be a good parent. There's no one-size-fits-all blueprint that works for every family in every situation. But are there priorities in parenting that Christian mothers and fathers should follow?

Paul outlined a Christian approach to parenting in the book of Ephesians:

> Children, obey your parents in the Lord, for this is right. "Honor your father and mother" (this is the first commandment with a promise), "that it may be well with you and that you may live long on the earth." Fathers, do not provoke your children to anger, but bring them up in the discipline and instruction of the Lord (Eph. 6:1-4).

As parents, how do we bring up our children in the discipline and instruction of the Lord? I believe there are three essential principles of godly parenting that address the key issues of faith, character and vision. I believe that if you focus on these three things, you and your kids will turn out all right. Plus, as you will see later in the chapter, you can even invite interesting people like Gandhi, Mozart, Malcolm X and Private Ryan to assist you, much as I utilized movies about these people to talk to my own children about their core beliefs and values.

1. Be Involved (but Not Anxious) About Evangelizing and Discipling Your Child

I am a living, breathing billboard for parents who raise their children in the discipline and instruction of the Lord. At the age of five, I knelt by my mother's side in our California home and asked Jesus into my heart.

My mother didn't have a theology degree, but she loved Jesus and she loved me. She explained to me the good news of the gospel of Jesus Christ. She explained to me how Jesus Christ died for my sins on Calvary's cross, how He paid the penalty for my sin. She explained to me how Jesus Christ rose from the dead and is alive, and He offers eternal life in heaven itself to all who believe in Him. She invited me to ask Jesus into my heart and life, trusting Him as Savior from sin and committing my life to Him as Lord.

Being Christians was more than just words for my mother and father. From the time I was born, they took me to church (first to Hollywood Presbyterian Church, and later to Glendale Presbyterian Church). But their responsibilities as Christian parents certainly didn't end at the church door. They talked to me throughout the week about how their faith impacted every aspect of their lives. We prayed together. We read the Bible together. After being around this kind of consistent testimony and lifestyle, it was only natural that I would want to ask Jesus into my heart and spend my life with Him.

My parents knew that the Great Commission was not just a concept or a rallying cry for big evangelistic campaigns. They knew they were supposed to fulfill the Great Commission in their home. Here's the way Jesus explained it in the final three verses of Matthew's Gospel:

> And Jesus came and said to them, "All authority in heaven and on earth has been given to me. Go therefore and

> make disciples of all nations, baptizing them in the name of the Father and of the Son and of the Holy Spirit, teaching them to observe all that I have commanded you; and lo, I am with you always, to the close of the age" (Matt. 28:18-20).

I want to focus on that line: "teaching them to observe all that I have commanded you." Many people think the Great Commission is all about evangelism. It is, particularly with its emphasis on "go." But our obligation doesn't stop there. Jesus is also urging all of us who are His disciples to help others become disciples of Jesus. My parents taught me to observe everything Jesus commanded. They didn't do so perfectly, but they did so intentionally and lovingly. Today, I am thankful for their example and their commitment to teaching, evangelizing and discipling me.

Not all moms or dads follow my parents' example. Some parents seem to follow the Charlemagne model. Charlemagne (or Charles the Great) was a powerful king and emperor who ruled much of Europe from 768 to 814. Some historians portray Charlemagne as a barbaric and violent man, while others see him as a committed Christian.

These two aspects of his character came together whenever his armies conquered opposing armies (which was fairly often). After his military victories, Charlemagne would have the defeated enemy soldiers do a strange thing. Those who had survived the battle were driven into water, whether that was in a nearby stream, lake or even the ocean. Why? Charlemagne wanted them to be baptized. In this unique post-victory ritual, he would "baptize" them forcibly, believing that if they were baptized, then they would be saved.

Today some churches still teach that baptism saves a child, and there are many parents who focus all their energies on getting their children baptized. For some, once a child's baptism has been accomplished, they breathe a big sigh of relief and focus on other matters.

My study of Scripture suggests that this approach is a grave misunderstanding of baptism. You cannot force someone to be baptized and thereby save them. Baptism can't save anybody. That's because baptism is a symbol, like a wedding ring. A wedding ring doesn't magically make two people married, but it symbolizes marriage, as baptism symbolizes salvation.

This reminds me of an embarrassing moment in my own marriage. I lost my wedding ring in 1979. It happened when I was in a theater watching the movie *Alien.* It was a scary movie, and I was nervous and fidgeting with my ring. I don't know whether it fell into a box of popcorn or just rolled down the aisle, but I was never able to find it. In time, I replaced that original wedding ring with the ring I wear today. But what about that period when I was without a ring? Did this mean I was not married? Hardly. I have been happily married since 1971. It's just that I went through a period when I was not wearing one of the most common symbols of marriage.

Don't get me wrong. Baptism is important. It's a sign of God's covenant to wash us and cleanse us of our sins, as well as a symbol of our commitment to God. It's just that baptism is not the sign that your mission as a parent is accomplished.

Your responsibility as a parent doesn't consist of delegating your children's spiritual growth to others. Church and youth group can help you, but there's more for you to do than dropping off Junior at church so that the teachers and the youth workers there can teach him, baptize him and save him.

You need to be heavily involved in evangelizing and discipling your children. In fact, if you don't take the lead in this process, it's difficult for a Sunday School teacher or youth worker to fill that void. No one can evangelize and disciple your children like you can. Those of us who serve in the church, in the Sunday School and in the youth group can certainly help you, but the work of "teaching them to observe all that I have commanded you" starts with you.

2. Concentrate on Character

Let's look back in history for a story I call "A Tale of Two Children." As our story opens, it's a decade before the twentieth century, and two children are about to be born on opposite sides of the earth. Each will change the world, but in dramatically different ways.

One child is born in Austria, in 1889, to an angry and bitter man who often beat his child. The mother was 23 years younger than the father and wanted to have nothing to do with motherhood. After the father died, the mother shipped the child off to an alcoholic aunt, where the child lived until he was 16 years of age. Unhappy with this arrangement, the child dropped out of high school and ran away from home. If this child was ever evangelized or discipled by any of the adults in his life, these efforts yielded little spiritual fruit.

As an adult, he joined the army and fought in World War I, but Austria's army was defeated and the entire nation was humiliated. These defeats inspired a successful career in politics. He was an expert at manipulating the feelings of inadequacy that he knew so well. In 1919, he founded the Nazi Party. The rest of the story is better known.

Imprisoned for political insurrection, he was released early by falsely promising that he would never again be involved in politics. In 1933, he was elected absolute ruler of the Germanic peoples. He declared himself Führer (which means leader). His military campaigns led much of the world into a brutal war, and he also killed off six million Jews before dying at his own hand in 1945, as the tattered remains of his short-lived Reich crumbled around him. That man was Adolf Hitler, and his career made him one of the most despised people who ever lived.

The other child was born in 1890, to a Christian family in the little town of Denison, Texas. His parents had been discipled by their parents, and now their number one goal was to disciple their beloved baby boy. When the child was two years of age, they moved to Kansas, where they joined the Church of the Brethren. They took the child to church every week, and at home, mom took time every day to find a quiet place to read and study the Bible with him and pray with him.

Accepted into West Point and later commissioned as a U.S. Army officer, he rose through the ranks until he was named the Supreme Commander of the Allied Forces in Europe, in 1943. On June 6, 1944, he successfully organized and commanded the Allied invasion of Europe. In 1952, he was elected the thirty-fourth President of the United States, serving two terms.

In 1969, ill and nearing death, he invited Billy Graham to sit by his bedside at Walter Reed Army Medical Center. The two men read the Bible, and then held hands and prayed together. Then the man said, "I'm ready," and left this world. The world mourned the passing of a powerful leader, Dwight David Eisenhower.

The contrast between these two men, born only a year apart, is dramatic, but the lesson is clear: The outcome of a child's life is largely influenced by what he or she receives in the home. Here's how the Bible states this principle:

> Train up a child in the way he should go, and when he is old he will not depart from it (Prov. 22:6).

Are there exceptions to this principle? Of course, but it remains the best principle for parents who care about the spiritual lives of their children. Parents have a huge influence on the character of their children.

What do you teach your children about the meaning and purpose of their existence? What do you convey to them about what makes life worth living? Is it business success and financial security? Is it fame and celebrity? Is it a lawn without a single weed and a family room without a speck of dust? Whatever it is you truly consider most important in life, you can count on this: Your children will figure it out.

If you want some guidance in determining how to teach your children to become men and women of character, follow the advice of the Early Church, which developed the following list of the seven deadly sins:

- Covetousness
- Lust
- Anger
- Pride
- Gluttony
- Envy
- Sloth

These seven sins, which cover the bad behavior we want to avoid, are paired with the seven cardinal virtues:

- Faith
- Hope
- Love
- Courage
- Justice
- Prudence
- Temperance

Interestingly, Paul also highlights these 14 sins and virtues, contrasting the "works of the flesh" with the "fruit of the Spirit":

> But I say, walk by the Spirit, and do not gratify the desires of the flesh.
>
> For the desires of the flesh are against the Spirit, and the desires of the Spirit are against the flesh; for these are opposed to each other, to prevent you from doing what you would. But if you are led by the Spirit you are not under the law.
>
> Now the works of the flesh are plain: fornication, impurity, licentiousness, idolatry, sorcery, enmity, strife, jealousy, anger, selfishness, dissension, party spirit, envy, drunkenness, carousing, and the like. I warn you, as I warned you before, that those who do such things shall not inherit the kingdom of God.
>
> But the fruit of the Spirit is love, joy, peace, patience, kindness, goodness, faithfulness, gentleness, self-control; against such there is no law. And those who belong to Christ Jesus have crucified the flesh with its passions and desires (Gal. 5:16-24).

We live in a world that desperately needs people of character. The sad thing is that many moms and dads are focused on other goals for their children. How can I say that? Because I see many parents who are primarily concerned with the kinds of practical knowledge and vocational skills that will help them "get ahead." They want their kids to get a good education and have a great career; and in some cases, character is farther down on the priority list.

Both Hitler and Eisenhower possessed knowledge and skills, but it was character that led each to use his knowledge and skills as he did: one for destructive ends and the other for constructive ends.

Are you a parent who loves God and loves your children? Then concentrate on character. You will be glad you did, and so will all of us who interact with your children in the future!

3. Broaden Your Child's Vision

In the leadership chapter of this book, I explained how a leader must be a vision caster. The same is true for parents, for parenting is just another form of leadership. Let me explain.

A few years ago, when Barb and I were in Detroit to attend a meeting of our denomination, we visited the Henry Ford Museum. One of the treasures in the museum was an old city bus built in 1948. This was the bus in which a young woman named Rosa Parks changed history by refusing to give up her seat. Barb and I took turns sitting in that old bus seat and thinking about how our world has changed.

You know the story about Rosa Parks. In 1955, she was waiting at a bus stop in Montgomery, Alabama. She entered the bus and entered history. At that time, African Americans were forced to sit in the back of the bus so that white people could have the better seats up front. But on December 1, 1955, the back of the bus was already full, so Rosa Parks sat in a seat closer to the middle of the bus. This was permissible as long as no whites wanted her seat; but when more whites entered the bus and the bus driver asked her to move, she declined to move and stayed where she was.

From a distance, this seems like a simple act. But her refusal to continue putting up with racial discrimination was both radical and risky. She was arrested and thrown into jail. Instead of letting this injustice continue, a group of 45 Montgomery pastors and preachers got together and organized a boycott of the Montgomery bus system. Their leader was a young, new minister named Martin Luther King, Jr.

The boycott was rough on Birmingham's blacks, most of whom depended on the public bus system to get to and from their low-paying jobs. But they were united in their dedication, and most of them simply got up earlier to walk to work or find a ride from fellow boycotters.

All of this history rushed in upon Barb and me as we took turns sitting in the seat where Rosa Parks had bravely sat. I thanked God for Rosa Parks's bravery and boldness. But as I sat there, I also sent up a silent prayer to God, asking, *Who will be the Rosa Parks of the next generation?* Who knows what challenges and injustices people will face in the future? That's why we need more people like Rosa Parks, and that's why you need to broaden your children's vision.

There's no such thing as a perfect child, but the parents of Christina-Taylor Green say their nine-year-old daughter was pretty close. It was Christina-Taylor's desire to create a better world that inspired her interest in politics, an interest that led her to a public meeting featuring Congresswoman Gabrielle Giffords of Arizona, a member of the United States House of

Representatives. Christina-Taylor wanted to ask the congresswoman's advice about how she could enter politics. As you remember, Giffords was shot and seriously injured at the rally on January 8, 2011. Christina-Taylor was killed.

Amid their grief and sorrow, her parents expressed their thankfulness for their daughter and her commitment to a better world.

Do you have a vision for your children that is as big and as broad as God's world?

Our church has a fourfold vision statement designed to inspire and guide everything we do. We desire to be "a congregation mobilized in service, to transform our community, elevate the urban poor, and impact our nation and world for Christ." This means that none of us should sit around, waiting for others to carry the load. Each and every one of us is to be mobilized in service and ministry for eternal purposes, serving the kingdom of heaven on earth. We regularly share this vision with our children in Sunday School in the hopes that some of them will embrace it for themselves.

What are you doing to broaden your children's vision? I know some parents who take their kids to work alongside them at a local soup kitchen for the poor and the homeless. Others take daughters and sons on mission trips so that they can see what happens in ministry at close range.

Children are capable of amazing things. Are you a helicopter parent who tries to keep your kids safe and secure, or are you willing to let God grab hold of your kids and transform them into a future Dwight Eisenhower or a future Rosa Parks?

How big is your vision for your kids, and how can you help them have big visions, too?

Don't Forget to Take It Easy!

Parenting is an awesome responsibility, but you don't need to be anxious about it. Some parents fear that in order to evangelize, disciple, train and inspire their children, they need to suddenly become theologians, pastors, psychologists, educators and drill sergeants. Perhaps these skills might help, but all you really need to be a successful and influential parent is to focus on what you know, and be consistent about it. Let me illustrate with an example from my own life.

I am a movie buff, and I love watching movies and then discussing them afterwards. This passion of mine was the inspiration for regular, weekly date nights that I had with my son and daughter. For years, we would choose a night for our date, and then we would watch a new movie in a theater and discuss it together over dinner at a restaurant.

This may sound simple, but it led to some of the most profound experiences the three of us ever shared. As we ate dinner together and excitedly discussed movies like *Star Wars, E.T. The Extra-Terrestrial, Schindler's List, Saving Private Ryan, The Shawshank Redemption, Blade Runner, Raiders of the Lost Ark, Malcolm X, Amadeus, Gandhi* and *The Elephant Man*, we found plenty of moral, spiritual and theological issues to debate.

I believe that movies are the stories of our age, and I love using movie discussions to go deep and look at things like the characters' beliefs and worldviews. Plus, some of the best movies also provide wonderful teaching opportunities.

Frankly, I never thought I was doing anything amazing by organizing these evenings with my two kids; but recently, I was talking to my daughter, and she said those outings were one of her favorite experiences growing up. I know that our habit of watching movies together and discussing them afterwards meant that my kids would look at movies more critically than other kids. But our discussions also enabled us to discuss issues that dealt directly with issues of discipleship, character and vision.

So, parents, I want you to be serious about discipling your children and teaching them to observe all that Jesus has commanded; but do it with love and grace. You don't need to memorize the Bible or be the world's best teacher to disciple your children.

In the long run, your sense of purpose, love and intentionality will outweigh your inadequacies and mistakes. God doesn't expect parents to be perfect, but He does command us to take seriously our role as our children's most powerful spiritual influence.

Reflection Questions

1. What do you think your children would say is the most important thing in your life? If possible, ask them directly to answer this question.

2. Define in a sentence or two what deep down you really want for your kids. As you honestly think about your answer, does your desire reflect the standards and ways of our culture, your own desires, or God's standards?

3. Have you ever had a conversation with your children about developing a faith or belief in God? If not, think through how and when you could do that.

4. How could you more consistently model the character of Christ to your children? What are one or two areas of growth as a parent that you could focus on in the months ahead?

5. How can you instruct your children in godly behavior while at the same time modeling grace, mercy and forgiveness?

6. If there was one thing you could change about your parenting style, what would it be? What would help you effectively implement that change?

7. What is one practice you could start with each of your children that would allow you to engage their hearts and minds in meaningful connection and communication?

Note

1. Nancy Gibbs, "The Growing Backlash Against Overparenting," *TIME,* November 30, 2009. http://www.time.com/time/magazine/article/0,9171,1940697,00.html.

5

What Kind of Leader Are You?

What do you think of when you hear the word "leader"? Who is the first person that pops into your mind? George Washington? Abraham Lincoln? Winston Churchill? Martin Luther King, Jr.? Napoleon?

Or perhaps you think of *poor* leaders, in which case the Congress of the United States may be at the top of your list. As I write these words, more than 80 percent of Americans disapprove of Congress's performance. I pray for these leaders regularly, as the Bible commands.

Do you think of yourself as a leader? I hope so, because I believe that Jesus wants *all* of His disciples to be leaders in their families and homes, their communities and schools, their churches and ministries, and in their neighborhoods and communities. This includes you. That's why I didn't use the following titles for this chapter:

"Are You a Leader?"

"Do You Have What It Takes to Be a Leader?"

I am starting with the assumption that you already are a leader. You may not be destined to be the president of a country or the CEO of a corporation, but you have an impact with others. My goal in this chapter is to help you become the leader God created you to be. Let's start by reviewing one of Jesus' most powerful lessons on leadership.

Leadership Upside Down

In 2010, as I was preparing to preach on the topic of leadership, George Steinbrenner died at the age of 80. Steinbrenner had been the owner of the New York Yankees, and he was a very powerful leader in the world of pro sports.

Steinbrenner's leadership style was of the top-down, my-way-or-the-highway variety. When he was asked about his philosophy of leadership, he said, "There are two types of leaders in the world. There are Pattons and there are Eisenhowers. I am a Patton."

He was referring to George S. Patton, the autocratic World War II commander, and Dwight D. Eisenhower, the more easy-going former commander who became the thirty-fourth president of the United States. Patton liberated more lands and captured more prisoners than any other leader in history, but his career was dogged by complaints that he was too hard on the soldiers who served under him. Eisenhower, on the other hand, was more laid-back. He was a strong leader, but he tried harder to build consensus among his followers instead of trampling over them, like Patton sometimes did.

As I think about the leaders I have worked with over the years, Steinbrenner had a valid point. But his dichotomy between dictators and team builders seems overly simplistic. Most of the truly great leaders have combined these two traits. They have known when to dictate and when to build consensus. They have known when to be democratic and when to be autocratic.

Are these two models the only choices we have as we consider the question of this chapter? Not according to Jesus, who presented His own leadership philosophy to His disciples as they squabbled with each other for prominence among the disciples:

> Then the mother of the sons of Zeb'edee came up to him, with her sons, and kneeling before him she asked him for something. And he said to her, "What do you want?" She said to him, "Command that these two sons of mine may sit, one at your right hand and one at your left, in your kingdom."
>
> But Jesus answered, "You do not know what you are asking. Are you able to drink the cup that I am to drink?"
>
> They said to him, "We are able."

> He said to them, "You will drink my cup, but to sit at my right hand and at my left is not mine to grant, but it is for those for whom it has been prepared by my Father."
>
> And when the ten heard it, they were indignant at the two brothers. But Jesus called them to him and said, "You know that the rulers of the Gentiles lord it over them, and their great men exercise authority over them. It shall not be so among you; but whoever would be great among you must be your servant, and whoever would be first among you must be your slave; even as the Son of man came not to be served but to serve, and to give his life as a ransom for many" (Matt. 20:20-28).

The Bible is not a leadership manual, but it does shine a light on the kind of leaders God wants us to be by exploring three core characteristics of a good leader.

1. The Good Leader Is a Servant Leader

There's a powerful scene in the first *Lord of the Rings* movie that captures the meaning of servant leadership. Everyone knows Middle Earth is under threat, but nobody knows what to do or how to respond. Various leaders are arguing and posturing, trying to make their points and pursue their agendas. Then, out of nowhere, comes a humble Hobbit named Frodo Baggins, who steps up and says, "Here am I, send me."

Frodo knew that the mission to capture the missing ring would be dangerous, perhaps even fatal. He knew that others in the room were much better warriors. But these concerns could not outweigh the one thing that is fundamental to good leaders: he was willing to serve.

We can certainly understand what motivated the mother of James and John. Which mother doesn't want the best for her children? But her request that her sons would be Jesus' top lieutenants reveals a serious misunderstanding about leadership that confuses many of us today. We think of leaders as people who sit at the top of the power pyramid and call all the shots. Jesus' view of leadership is just the opposite. Good leaders are humble and lowly. They are more concerned with serving others than getting their own way.

If the Matthew passage allows us to understand Jesus' philosophy of leadership, a passage in John's gospel shows Him putting that philosophy into action in a surprising way:

> Jesus, knowing that the Father had given all things into his hands, and that he had come from God and was going to God, rose from supper, laid aside his garments, and girded himself with a towel. Then he poured water into a basin, and began to wash the disciples' feet, and to wipe them with the towel with which he was girded (John 13:3-5).

Chapters 13–17 of the Gospel of John are often called the Upper Room Discourse. Jesus would soon be crucified, so He gathered His disciples together for one last meal before He concluded His earthly ministry. It is in the Upper Room that Jesus institutes the Lord's Supper, or Eucharist, a ritual that Christians around the world have observed ever since.

Foot washing is also a regular ritual today in some churches, even though we don't have the problem with dirty feet that was the norm in Jesus' day. Towns and villages didn't have sidewalks or pedestrian plazas, and people didn't have the kinds of shoes and socks that today protect our feet from dirt and grime.

Back then nearly everyone wore sandals as they walked on rocks, dust, cobblestones and dirt. When it was time to visit someone's home, the first thing a gracious host did when guests arrived was to order the servants or slaves of the house to wash the guests' feet. It was a dirty, horrible and thankless job, and nobody but the lowest of the low did it. This helps us see how radical it was for Jesus to do what He did.

Always the teacher, Jesus explained His actions after He completed washing His disciples' feet:

> When he had washed their feet, and taken his garments, and resumed his place, he said to them, "Do you know what I have done to you? You call me Teacher and Lord; and you are right, for so I am. If I then, your Lord and Teacher, have washed your feet, you also ought to wash one another's feet. For I have given you an example, that you also should do as I have done to you. Truly, truly, I say to you, a servant is not greater than his master; nor is he who is sent greater than he who sent him. If you know these things, blessed are you if you do them" (John 13:12-17).

Do you want to be a good leader? Then you must be a servant leader. This means that you need to be like Frodo: willing to step forward and serve, even when you're scared and the outcome is in doubt. It means you need to be like Jesus, the Savior of the world, who demonstrated His love by becoming a lowly servant to His disciples.

2. The Good Leader Delegates

One of the most ancient leadership lessons in human history comes from the book of Exodus, which describes the Jews' journey from captivity in Egypt to the Promised Land of Israel.

Can you imagine hundreds of thousands—perhaps even millions—of people hiking across the desert, month after month? Imagine all the issues and complaints their leader, Moses, dealt with. It was clear to Moses' father-in-law, Jethro, that this was an impossible situation:

> On the morrow Moses sat to judge the people, and the people stood about Moses from morning till evening.
>
> When Moses' father-in-law saw all that he was doing for the people, he said, "What is this that you are doing for the people? Why do you sit alone, and all the people stand about you from morning till evening?"
>
> And Moses said to his father-in-law, "Because the people come to me to inquire of God; when they have a dispute, they come to me and I decide between a man and his neighbor, and I make them know the statutes of God and his decisions."

Moses' father-in-law said to him, "What you are doing is not good. You and the people with you will wear yourselves out, for the thing is too heavy for you; you are not able to perform it alone. Listen now to my voice; I will give you counsel, and God be with you! You shall represent the people before God, and bring their cases to God; and you shall teach them the statutes and the decisions, and make them know the way in which they must walk and what they must do. Moreover choose able men from all the people, such as fear God, men who are trustworthy and who hate a bribe; and place such men over the people as rulers of thousands, of hundreds, of fifties, and of tens. And let them judge the people at all times; every great matter they shall bring to you, but any small matter they shall decide themselves; so it will be easier for you, and they will bear the burden with you. If you do this, and God so commands you, then you will be able to endure, and all this people also will go to their place in peace."

So Moses gave heed to the voice of his father-in-law and did all that he had said. Moses chose able men out of all Israel, and made them heads over the people, rulers of thousands, of hundreds, of fifties, and of tens. And they judged the people at all times; hard cases they brought to Moses, but any small matter they decided themselves. Then Moses let his father-in-law depart, and he went his way to his own country (Exod. 18:13-27).

Moses was an extremely reluctant leader. Back in Exodus 3, God called Moses to lead the Jews out of Egypt, but Moses wasn't excited about this new assignment, and he tried to get out of it by asking God, "Who am I that I should go to Pharaoh, and bring the sons of Israel out of Egypt?" (Exod. 3:11). In other words: God, can You send someone else?

But God often chooses unlikely people to serve Him. God commissioned Moses to lead the exodus from Egypt and promised to be with him and guide him every step of the way.

Today, many people become leaders reluctantly. They don't want to be in the spotlight or on the firing line, but they emerge as leaders because their sense of service or passion or calling overcomes their reluctance. That's what happened to Moses, who needed to continually grow in his leadership abilities.

The lesson Jethro spoke to Moses was to delegate. Instead of doing everything himself, Moses needed to appoint others to handle some tasks so that he could focus on the things that were more important.

Where would companies like Apple and Microsoft be without delegation? There probably wouldn't be an Apple or a Microsoft, just Steve Jobs and Bill Gates sitting in a California garage, tinkering with computer circuits instead of handing off these duties so that they could focus on growing massive global corporations.

Are you the kind of person who likes to have your hand on all the details so that you can make sure everything is done perfectly? If so, this attitude will severely limit your abilities as a leader.

Is God calling you to lead? If so, that calling may come with the requirement that you learn to delegate. Try it, and in time you might begin to enjoy the contributions others can make. That's key to being a good leader.

3. The Good Leader Casts a Vision

The Old Testament book of Proverbs states a powerful truth: "Where there is no vision, the people perish" (Prov. 29:18, *KJV*). *THE MESSAGE*, a more recent translation, expresses the same truth in different words: "If people can't see what God is doing, they stumble all over themselves."

A good leader must cast a vision so that people can understand what the goal is and how it will be achieved. The better the leader, the more people will be able to feel the goal in their hearts and envision it in their imaginations.

Jesus was probably the greatest vision caster and greatest leader the world has ever known. What was the vision Jesus cast for His followers? It was the kingdom of God. And how did He cast this vision? His primary method was through His many parables.

Parables have been defined as earthly stories containing spiritual truths. Jesus told nearly 50 different parables, many of them beginning with the phrase "the kingdom of heaven is like . . ." or "the kingdom of heaven may be compared to . . ." Jesus painted a picture of the kingdom of God by creating stories about the lost sheep, the prodigal son, the unforgiving servant, the lamp under a bushel, and other powerful stories.

There were times when the disciples were confused by these parables. For example, following His teaching on the sower and the seed (see Matt. 13:1-9), Jesus' disciples asked, "'Why do you speak to the people in parables?' He replied, 'Because the knowledge of the secrets of the kingdom of heaven has been given to you'" (Matt. 13:10-11, *NIV*).

Jesus wanted His parables to help us understand the character of the kingdom of God, the character of the King, and the character of those who are citizens in the kingdom of God. For instance, in parables like the mustard seed, we learn that the Kingdom is meant to grow like the mustard seed, which is the smallest of all seeds but grows into the greatest of shrubs. In this way is the kingdom of God destined to grow in this world.

In the parable of the leaven, we are taught that the kingdom of God is meant to grow within each one of us so that it will infuse and infiltrate us in the midst of our corruption and fallenness, and transform us, much like leavening agents in dough make bread rise.

We learn about the character of the King (God) in the parables of the prodigal son and the lost coin, which show us that God has come to save and seek the lost. In the parable of the workers in the vineyard, we see that it is the character of the King to save all who seek salvation, whether you come to the vineyard early in the day or late in the day; whether you come to know Jesus early in your life or late in your life. Regardless of our behavior or devotion, the character of the King is to save us.

We learn about the character of the Kingdom's subjects in the parable of the Good Samaritan, which shows that Kingdom people are to be people of compassion. The parable of the persistent widow teaches that those who belong to the kingdom of God are to be passionate and persistent in prayer. In the parable of the talents and the parable of the pound, we see that citizens of the kingdom of God are good stewards. We know that the King owns everything, and we are His loyal and faithful stewards. We are called to use all of our time, all of our talent, all of our treasure in the service of the King.

Can you see what I mean about the leadership approach of Jesus? Jesus is a leader who casts a vision, and it is a vision of the kingdom of God. As you seek to serve God by being a leader, focus on casting a vision that is compelling and clear.

Help Wanted: Good Leaders

We've seen what happens when leaders can't lead. It's similar to trying to captain a ship without a rudder: the ship goes around and around in circles until it sinks to the bottom of the sea. That's why I want to issue a Help Wanted search for leaders. Are you interested in applying?

We need leaders who will provide leadership in the home, helping children and adults serve and love each other.

We need leaders who will provide leadership in the church, helping children come to know the heavenly Father, and guiding adults toward Kingdom living in all aspects of their lives.

We need leaders in business, law, commerce, technology and every other field known to the human race. We need professional leaders who will care for employees and serve owners while ensuring that companies and corporations act in accordance not only to worldly laws but also to Kingdom values.

As we know so well, we need leaders in government—from the local level to the halls of Washington and the United Nations. We need leaders who have a keen grasp of the nature of God's kingdom and will do everything they can to make our chaotic and broken world more aligned with the nature of this heavenly Kingdom every day of their lives.

Finally, we need leaders who will serve as beacons of light in a world that can too often become enveloped in darkness. The cause of the kingdom of God has been placed before us. Nothing is more important. Jesus taught us about this Kingdom in His parables, His discourses and in His counsel on how to pray.

We live in a critical hour and a critical time. The call for leaders is great. Are you willing to lead? If so, that willingness—combined with continuing growth in the skills of servant leadership, delegation and vision casting—can enable you to do great things in life.

Reflection Questions

1. What has been your best experience of good leadership? What made it good?

2. Based on your own life experience, do you tend to identify with General Patton's autocratic way of leading, or President Eisenhower's consensus leadership style, or do you fall somewhere in-between? Why?

3. How does Jesus' definition of leadership vary from your style of leadership? In what ways could you become more of a servant leader?

4. Do you find it easy to delegate responsibilities to others? Why or why not?

5. List some benefits of delegating tasks and responsibilities to others. What are some of the consequences of trying to do everything on your own?

6. In the areas of your life where you provide some kind of leadership, how can you become a better vision caster? Where does God want you to lead others? How can you get there?

7. What is one practical take-away from this chapter that will help you become a better overall leader?

6

Your Legacy?

My father, Ford Stanton Dixon, died in 1996. He was a CPA who worked as a supervising auditor for California's State Board of Equalization. His biggest brush with public fame probably happened when he audited the tax returns of Disneyland; but those who knew him privately remember a man of deep faith who loved to laugh and who was always telling interesting stories.

Today, when I look out of my office window at the church, I can see Mount Falcon in the distance. My father and I hiked that Colorado mountain when he was in his 70s, just as we had hiked many other mountains in California as I was growing up. We would regularly go for daylong hikes, often joined by my brothers and some of our friends. In one case, we embarked upon a weeklong, 100-mile backpacking trip on the John Muir Trail.

I have many warm memories about those hikes through California's beautiful wilderness areas, but one thing sticks out in my mind: my father's infectious love for creation. When we took a water break along the trail, or when we sat around the campfire at night, he would survey our surroundings and ask us, "Have you ever seen anything more beautiful than this?" Today, when I am out in nature, or even when I am looking out my office window, I still view the world through my father's eyes—eyes that saw the majesty of the Creator in the beauty of creation. For me, and for my brothers and our many hiking companions, this is merely one aspect of my father's legacy.

What do you think of when you consider the concept of legacy? There's a historic definition of legacy (where we talk about the ancient Romans and Greeks, and the lessons they handed down to us). There is also a personal approach toward legacy. What will be your legacy? After you have left this world, what will you leave with the friends and family members who knew you and loved you? Will you leave a legacy to the future? Or will all traces of your life pass away, like footprints on a sandy beach that are washed away by the ebb and flow of the waves?

Most of the time, it seems as if we are too preoccupied with the present to consider our legacy in the future. But there's one thing that almost never fails to shake people up and make people think long and hard about their legacy: attending someone else's funeral.

I have participated in a fair number of funerals for family members and members of our church. It's always amazing to watch the people who attend the funeral. What do they say about the loved one who has died? How do they react to the eulogy that summarizes the deceased's life and impact?

For many people, their primary legacy will be seen in the lives of their children. But you will create a legacy regardless of whether you have children.

In this chapter, I want to focus on three concepts that will determine the kind of legacy you leave: memory, example and work. Let's examine each concept to see how you can be intentional about creating the kind of legacy that is worthy of your life.

1. Meaningful Memories Make a Legacy

The power of memories was explored in a 1987 movie called *Throw Momma from the Train.* It's a horrible title, and the move itself isn't great. But I can still recall one powerful scene in which Danny DeVito (who plays a depressed mama's boy named Owen) shows his unusual coin collection to Billy Crystal (who plays Larry, a frustrated writing professor). Their discussion about the coin collection focuses on what makes something truly worthwhile and memorable.

Owen: Do you want to see my coin collection?
Larry: No.
Owen: I collect coins. I've got a dandy collection.
Larry: I don't want to see it, Owen.
Owen: But it's my collection.
Larry: I don't care. Look, Owen, I'm just not in the mood, okay?

Owen: I've never showed it to anyone before.

Larry: All right. I'll look at it.

Owen: No, that's okay.

Larry: Show me the collection.

Owen: No, you don't mean it.

Larry: Show me the coins!

Owen: All right. This one is a nickel. This one also is a nickel. And here's a quarter and another quarter and a penny. See, nickel, nickel, quarter, quarter, penny.

Larry: Are any of these coins worth anything?

Owen: No. And here is another nickel.

Larry: Why do you have them?

Owen: What do you mean?

Larry: Well, the purpose of a coin collection is that the coins are worth something, Owen.

Owen: Oh, but they are. This one here I got in change when my dad took me to see Peter, Paul and Mary. This one I got in change when I bought a hot dog at the circus. My daddy let me keep the change. He always let me keep the change. This one is my favorite. This is Martin & Lewis at the Hollywood Palladium. Look at that. See the way it shines on the little eagle? I loved my dad a lot.

Larry: So this whole collection is . . .

Owen: Change my daddy left me.

Larry: What was his name?

Owen: Ned. He used to call me "His little Ned." I really miss him.

Larry: That's a real nice collection, Owen.
Owen: Thank you, Larry . . .

Owen wasn't a numismatist (that's a fancy word for coin collector). So what was it that made his coins so valuable to him? It wasn't their rarity. These were common, everyday coins. They had no uniqueness that would increase their value.

These coins were valuable to Owen because they were associated with warm memories of times he had spent with his father before his father died. This scene works because it shows that a big part of building a legacy is making memories.

Jesus knew that making memories was a huge part of leaving a legacy. Before His crucifixion, He told His disciples that after He left He would send to them the Holy Spirit, who would bring to their remembrance all that Jesus had said and done so that His legacy would live on in the memories of those who knew Him and followed Him. One of the things they would remember was the Last Supper Jesus had with His disciples.

The night before Jesus went to the cross, He instituted the sacrament of Communion with these simple words: "Do this in remembrance of me" (Luke 22:19). This simple ceremony, which was first celebrated with a small group of confused and anxious disciples, is now celebrated by a billion believers around the world, in churches big and small. Jesus wanted us to remember Him and reflect on His love and mercy, so He created a ritual that would help us remember.

Today you have been given 86,400 seconds to spend any way you like. You will be given another 86,400 seconds tomorrow, and the next day, and the next. That's 604,800 seconds this week. Or more than 18 million seconds this month. Or more than two billion seconds this year.

Once these seconds are gone, you can't get them back. They are like grains of sand passing through an hourglass. What will you do today and tomorrow to make the seconds of your life meaningful to you and to others in the future? What choices will you make about the time you have to ensure that your legacy is one that matters? Answering questions like these is what it means to make a legacy.

2. Your Example Is Your Legacy

You've probably heard of Karl Marx. Marx was born in 1818, and by the time he died 64 years later, he had left his mark on the world through his philosophical writings, his sociological analysis of nations and their economies, and in his best-known written work, *The Communist Manifesto*, which helped give birth to both the Socialist and Communist movements that impacted Europe and the world during the nineteenth and twentieth centuries.

Marx wrote and spoke millions of words, but he is often remembered for one simple sentence consisting of seven words and twelve syllables: "Religion is the opiate of the masses."

The sentence came from one of Marx's earliest works, *Critique of Hegel's Philosophy of Right*, which he wrote when he was 30 years old. Here are the sentences that preceded his famous quote: "Religion is the sigh of the hard-pressed creature. It is the heart of a heartless world. It is the soul of soulless circumstances."

How could a man who descended from a long line of Jewish rabbis develop such a negative and pragmatic approach to religion? The answer can be found in the examples Marx saw around him. In particular, his father, Hirschel, did not provide a very good example of religious commitment and devotion.

Marx's father was a complicated man. He was relatively prosperous, which meant the family could live in a middle-class area of Germany. Karl attended synagogue every week with his father, but his father did not actually believe in God. For him, religion was more of a family and social obligation. Hirschel was probably an atheist. He had memorized most of the works of French philosopher Voltaire, and celebrated the ideas of the Enlightenment, which attacked religious belief as silly and harmful.

Then something interesting happened that brought about a big change in the family. As Hirschel's business connections grew and he felt even more pressure to conform to community norms, he announced that he was converting to Lutheranism and began taking Karl to a Lutheran church. Can you imagine how stunned the family was by this shift in religious loyalties?

With an example like this, how could Karl Marx view religion as something real and genuine? Hirschel Marx's religious behavior is a perfect example of hypocrisy, which is defined as "the practice of claiming to have moral standards or beliefs to which one's own behavior does not conform." Today when people think of hypocrisy, they point to the public failures of religious leaders who preach one thing and do another, or to political leaders who flip flop by changing their positions in order to gain a few more votes. Karl Marx's experience shows that private hypocrisy can be equally devastating.

What kind of example are you setting for the people who look up to you? Are you an elder at your church on Sundays, but Monday through Friday you demean your fellow workers while helping your company skirt government regulations or take accounting shortcuts?

Do you teach lessons about Christian living at Sunday School that you violate in your private life?

Do you talk about the need for integrity among politicians and public servants while you cheat on your income taxes?

Do you say that the most important thing in life is relationships but you spend every available hour at the office?

You are constructing your legacy every moment of every day, and it probably won't be based primarily on the words you say. It will be based on what you do. It's what people see, not what you say, that creates your example. And the example you give is one of the most important aspects of your legacy.

3. Your Work Is Your Legacy

Time was running out for Jesus. After three years of teaching and healing and performing miracles, the hour of His death was approaching. In John 13–16, He had a final session with His disciples where He predicted both His coming betrayal by Judas and Peter's subsequent denial that he knew Jesus.

It was a tough meeting, but Jesus had more complicated news for His disciples. He would return at the end of the age to redeem them. Before His return they would face much persecution; but even during their most difficult moments, the Holy Spirit would be there to help them and strengthen them. After completing this final teaching session with His disciples, Jesus then turned His eyes to heaven and prayed to His Father:

> I glorified thee on earth, having accomplished the work which thou gravest me to do; and now, Father, glorify thou me in thy own presence with the glory which I had with thee before the world was made (John 17:4-5).

When Jesus came into our world, He had important work to do. He was sent to earth for a special mission; and as He approached the final moments of His life, He could report to His father that this mission had been accomplished. What was Jesus' mission? Most theologians and Bible scholars say there are three aspects of the work Christ was sent here to do.

First, through His incarnation, Jesus came to show us the Father. Jesus is Immanuel, which means "God with us." Jesus came to show us the Father so that we might know what God is like: "No one has ever seen God; the only Son, who is in the bosom of the Father, he has made him known" (John 1:18). That was His work, to show us the Father.

A second aspect of His work was to atone for human sin. This was His work of atonement. From Old Testament times, God had demanded atonement for sin (which means making amends or reparation for any injuries or wrongs committed). This work had been assigned to Jesus before His birth and foretold by prophets. An angel explained this work to Joseph, whose wife would soon give birth to the baby Jesus: "You shall call his name Jesus, for he will save his people from their sins" (Matt. 1:21). Jesus came to die for the sins of the world. That was the second component of His work; and as Jesus prayed to His Father, He knew that the second component of His work would be happening soon.

The third and final aspect of Christ's work was establishing His Church. Jesus told Peter, "On this rock I will build my church, and the powers of death shall not prevail against it" (Matt. 16:18). Jesus began this work of establishing His Church with His disciples, many of whom would become apostles and founders of the Christian Church that today has more than a billion members around the world.

What about you? Do you have a clear sense of the work you are to do during your time on earth? None of us is capable of doing the kind of work Jesus did; but doesn't each and every one of us have a special work to do that is part of what God had in mind for us from the time before we even existed?

What's your work? You might think, *Well, my work is my career. It's my job. It's where I go when I leave the house in the morning.* Certainly your job matters to God. Your career is part of your work on earth, and the services or products or resources you create are very important, but this doesn't capture all of what I mean when I talk about your work.

Perhaps you don't work outside the home; your work is in the home, loving and rearing your children and family while taking care of the many tasks that come with managing a household.

This work is very important, too, but work with family doesn't completely fulfill this important concept of work.

There's another form of work that is important to Christians who love God and seek to serve Him. For us, the supreme purpose of our existence in this world is our service to the kingdom of heaven. This is an important part of the work God would have us do. Jesus said, "Seek first his kingdom and his righteousness" (Matt. 6:33). This is our work: toiling alongside our fellow Christian brothers and sisters in the task of building God's kingdom.

I love how Paul expressed this in Ephesians 2:10: "For we are his workmanship, created in Christ Jesus for good works, which God prepared beforehand, that we should walk in them."

What is the work God has called you to do? That's a question you need to answer for yourself through practicing various tasks, as well as through prayer, reflection and meditation on God's Word. I can give you some ideas to help you in your journey. You can start by being more than a pew-sitter in your church; start by rolling up your sleeves and pitching in to serve Christ's Body on earth.

Building the church is something that all Christians must do. Church work is not solely the duty of the pastor and the staff. They certainly have their work to do, but the church is your duty, too. We're in this together. This is our work, and our legacy is tied to this.

Maybe you think you aren't spiritually mature enough to serve the church. Maybe you fear you are too weak or too unskilled. God understands your fears. He just doesn't want you to be dominated by them. Anyone who has ever worked in the church knows that not everyone who is involved is a saint. But they're committed and involved. That's a good start.

Maybe you're concerned that you won't be able to accomplish anything of lasting value for God, but the results are not yours to control. God doesn't demand that you produce phenomenal results, just that you faithfully listen for His call and respond in faith through your acts of service.

I once heard Rev. Robert Schuller of the Crystal Cathedral, in Southern California, preach on this topic of results. Schuller told the story of George Smith, a Moravian missionary who felt God had called him to take the gospel to a remote area of Africa. After years of preparation and much hard work among the African people, Smith became ill and was forced to return home, convinced that he had been a failure. After all, only one woman had responded to his messages about Jesus' love and salvation.

But Smith didn't need to worry about his results. Decades later, missionaries returned to this area of Africa. What they found there was shocking. Another 11,000 people had come to faith through the evangelism work that began with the one woman who had responded to Smith's gospel message. Mission accomplished!

At the conclusion of the sermon, Schuller said something pretty amazing: "Any fool can count the number of seeds in an apple. But only God knows the number of apples in a seed."

That's what I would like you to think about as you consider this concept of work. What is your work that God has called you to do? Only you and God can figure that out. But I encourage you to figure out what it is and start doing it today. I say that for your sake, as well as for everyone else's. You will never find the kind of fulfillment and meaning you seek in life until you discover the work God has for you. And as for the rest of us, we are depending on you to do the work that only you can accomplish!

A Lasting Legacy of Your Life

My heart overflows with memories about the many people whose legacies have impacted my life. Mel Zimmer and Norm Steen were two Sunday School teachers and youth group leaders at Glendale Presbyterian Church who taught me when I was young. They helped me understand many confusing things about the Bible and Christian teaching. Even more important, it seemed that they really liked me. Being around them made me feel good through and through. As they taught me about Jesus, I came to accept that Christ really loved me. Years later, when I was ordained to the ministry, I invited them to my ordination service and thanked them for their legacy in my life.

What about you and your legacy? Are you building memories? Are you providing an example that others can follow? Are you doing the work God has called you to do?

The apostle Paul could answer yes to all of these questions. He wasn't perfect, but he had left a legacy that Timothy and others could see and follow:

> Now you have observed my teaching, my conduct, my aim in life, my faith, my patience, my love, my steadfastness, my persecutions, my sufferings, what befell me at Antioch, at Ico'nium, and at Lystra, what persecutions I endured; yet from them all the Lord rescued me. Indeed all who desire to live a godly life in Christ Jesus will be persecuted, while evil men and impostors will go on from bad to worse, deceivers and deceived.
>
> But as for you, continue in what you have learned and have firmly believed, knowing from whom you learned it and how from childhood you have been acquainted with the sacred writings which are able to instruct you for salvation through faith in Christ Jesus (2 Tim. 3:10-15).

What kind of legacy are you creating? When your friends and loved ones are sitting at your funeral and remembering your life, what are the things they will think about? I hope it won't be the long hours you put in at your office or the possessions you purchased with the money you earned. Instead, I hope they will recall the many meaningful memories you left them; the powerful, positive example you were; and the lasting legacy you left for many.

Your legacy is the evidence of the life you live, and the only way to create a powerful legacy is to live the kind of life that will serve as a positive example to others.

Reflection Questions

1. How do you want to be remembered by others? What inscription would you want on your grave marker?

2. What are some practices you could incorporate into your life that would help create lasting memories? What could you incorporate into your home? At your workplace? At your place of volunteer service?

3. Are there any areas of your life where your walk is not matching your talk? If so, what changes will you make so that you can live a more consistent life of integrity?

4. Make a list of your gifts and talents (it might be helpful to think of what other people have recognized in you). Add to that list some of your desires concerning what you want to do in your life. Now look over your compiled list. What are some ways you could begin to use those gifts and desires in serving God? (Consider meeting with a church staff member to go over these items.)

5. Read Colossians 3:23-24. How could you go about your daily work/job in such a way that it would be done "as unto the Lord"?

7

Do You Have Time for God?

"Someday, if I ever have the time, I would like to . . ."

How many times have you heard people say this? Whether it's learning to square dance, finally reading *War and Peace,* or traveling to some of the destinations described in *1001 Places to Visit Before You Die,* it seems that for some of us, "someday" remains in the distant future.

That's why I find the story of Larry "lawn chair" Walters so fascinating. Larry had always wanted to fly. He had joined the Air Force, but his poor eyesight prevented him from being a pilot. Some days, Larry would sit in his lawn chair in front of his San Pedro, California, home, looking up into the sky where he could see the contrails made by jets far overhead. This only deepened his desire to fly.

One sunny July day in 1982, Larry decided to do something about it. He went to the local Army/Navy Surplus store where he purchased a large tank of helium. Next he purchased 45 weather balloons. Then he started filling the balloons with helium, until each one was four feet in diameter, and tying them to his lawn chair, which was tethered to the ground by a thick rope. Finally, he fixed himself a sandwich and a soft drink, grabbed his BB gun and settled into the lawn chair.

Larry had planned to cut the tether rope and glide up into the air where he could enjoy his snack. When he was ready to end his brief trip, he would use the BB gun to shoot the balloons and descend gently back to earth.

But things didn't work out as planned. Once the anchoring rope was severed, the lawn chair launched into the sky as if propelled by a rocket. Larry was shocked as the chair flew heavenward, eventually reaching an altitude of 15,000 feet before finally leveling out at around 11,000 feet.

He had finally achieved his dream of flying, but he was too terrified to enjoy it and so afraid of falling to earth that he couldn't take a shot at any of the balloons. After nearly 14 hours aloft, he drifted into the flight path at the Long Beach Airport, where an airline pilot saw him and radioed flight controllers. "You're not going to believe this," said the pilot, "but there's a man sitting in his lawn chair at 11,000 feet, and he has a gun in his lap!"

Authorities unsuccessfully tried to rescue Larry by using a helicopter. Eventually, enough helium leaked out of his balloons that he finally lost altitude, hit a power line (interrupting power to a Long Beach neighborhood) and fell to the ground, where officials stood waiting to arrest him for violating various air regulations.

Larry may not be an expert on aeronautics, but his exciting flight showed that he knew how to put a dream into action. "A man can't just sit around," said Larry to a curious reporter.

What about you? Have you always dreamed of flying, or speaking Russian or running a marathon? What prevents you from doing what you really want to do?

What Do *You* Really Want to Do?

I hear many people talk about wish lists and bucket lists. People also tell me about their desire to grow closer to God or serve Him more actively. They tell me, "Someday, if I ever have the time, I would like to pray more."

Or "I would like to read the Bible from beginning to end."

Or "I want to get more involved in a small group."

Or "I am going to devote time to serving the needy in my community."

Or "I would really like to teach a Sunday School class someday."

My response is to say something like this: "Someday can start today!" But it doesn't always happen that way. It often seems that "someday" never comes.

Why do so many people seem to have so little time for the things they say they want to do, including their spiritual goals in life? When it comes to doing the things that God wants us to do, why is it that some people seemingly choose to just "sit around"?

During my decades as a pastor, I have heard people offer every imaginable excuse for not attending church, for not reading the Bible or praying, for not volunteering in the community, or for not helping out at church. By far the most frequent excuse I hear is, "Gee, Pastor, I just don't have the time."

When I dig deeper, I discover that they seem to have plenty of time for other activities, such as attending sporting events. Denver is fortunate to have three great pro teams: the Broncos in football; the Nuggets in basketball; and the Avalanche in hockey. But when these teams have Sunday games, church attendance suffers.

I love the Broncos/Nuggets/Avalanche as much as the next person. But as a pastor, I have repeatedly been struck by how sports compete with church commitments for a share of people's time. The growing popularity of NFL football over the years has created challenges for people trying to find time for church or family on Sunday afternoons (and now Sunday evenings, as well as Monday nights, some Thursdays and other days during the season or 24/7 on the NFL cable channel). Football also has a significant impact on how many of us celebrate special holidays like Thanksgiving and Christmas. In some homes, the sound of the play-by-play commentary and the frequent commercials drowns out everything else.

Don't get me wrong. I'm not anti-football; I'm a Broncos fan myself. But sometimes I wonder if it wouldn't be better if millions of us spent more time being with each other or exercising our bodies, and less time watching millionaire athletes duke it out on the gridiron.

In the rest of this chapter, we will look at the problem of time. For most of us, it seems like we don't have enough of it. But in reality, we all have the same amount of time as the next person. It's all about how we use it.

Timely Ways to Measure Time

How often during an average day do you check to see what time it is? And how do you check it? Do you look at your wristwatch? Do you check your smart phone? Do you glance at a clock on a wall?

The ways that people measure and keep track of time have changed drastically over the last few millennia.

Some of the earliest methods humans used to measure time were Stonehenge in England and the Great Pyramid in Egypt. These were used to track seasons and years more than minutes and hours. Amazingly, ancient engineers were successful in building huge monuments that accurately predicted annual events like the winter solstice.

In the ancient world, people used sundials to help them determine what time it was (at least during daylight hours on sunny days).

Ancient people also measured time with a clepsydra, which is a fancy word for water clock. Water clocks regulated the flow of water—either into or out of a vessel—in order to keep track of the passing of time. These clocks were popular in ancient Egypt and Babylon, 16 centuries *before* Christ, and they remained in use until 16 centuries *after* Christ, with new engineering and adaptations being made throughout history. These clocks worked fairly well, but they were less accurate than modern clocks.

It wasn't until a thousand years after the death of Christ that inventors created the first mechanical clock, which used springs and gears and weights to keep track of time. Some historians give the credit to a monk named Gerbert of Aurillac, who would later become Pope Silvester II in AD 999.

One of the latest time-keeping developments is the invention of atomic clocks, which are based on atomic physics and the microwave signals that atoms emit. An atomic clock called FOCS 1 started operating in Switzerland in 2004, and scientists claim it will lose less than one second every 30 million years!

Humanity's devices for measuring time have changed over the millennia, but there are two things that haven't changed: how much time we have every day and what God wants us to do with it.

From Timely to Timeless

No matter how we measure it, there are still 24 hours in a day, which means that you and I have as much time in a day as our ancient ancestors did. That hasn't changed.

It may *seem* like we have less time, but that's because we try to cram so much frantic activity into every moment of every day that there's nothing left over. There's no margin. That's why people are so exhausted and stressed much of the time, and why they regularly say, "I just don't have the time."

Some say that the answer to the problem of time is multitasking—which involves doing more than one thing simultaneously. But brain scans show that we don't actually multitask as successfully as we think we do. Instead, the brain rapidly alternates between one activity and the other, toggling back and forth and actually *wasting* precious time in the process of trying to manage two simultaneous tasks.

The second thing that hasn't changed over the centuries is what matters to God. We are to love God and love our neighbor, and love requires time. In the sight of God, it's not very important how we measure time or what devices we use. The thing that's important is how we use the precious time we have been given.

It comes down to a matter of stewardship. If you have attended church for very long, you have heard the concept of stewardship applied mainly to money. But God calls us to be good stewards of everything we have been given, and that includes the time we are given each day and throughout our lives. Anybody can tell time, but it's a wise person who knows how to use time.

The concept of time stewardship can be found in a psalm of Moses:

> So teach us to number our days that we may get a heart of wisdom (Ps. 90:12).

I have frequently taught and preached on this psalm, but over the years something has changed in how I understand it.

The thing that has changed is *me*. I am getting older. Of course, each one of us is getting older every second of every day. But as I move through my sixties, the reality that I need to number my days has sunk into my consciousness on a much deeper level than ever before.

Whenever I hear myself thinking, *Someday, if I ever have the time, I would like to . . .* I immediately remind myself that someday needs to be today. I realize that my days are numbered. They are finite. My life will not stretch on into the future forever and ever. My time is now. Someday is today.

The Bible teaches that wise people have a good sense of time. They number their days. It's not about telling time; it's about using time. God wants us to know how to use time wisely. Is that what we do?

God Needs People Who Have Time to Serve

Every year the U.S. Department of Labor's Bureau of Labor Statistics releases a report on what Americans do with their time. Here is a look at how the average person spends time on various tasks and activities:

- Sleeping takes the biggest chunk of time, with the average American spending 8.67 hours a day sleeping. (If it seems like you don't ever get this much sleep in a day, remember your personal sleep hours have been averaged in with millions of other people, including toddlers and older people who sleep more than you do.)

- The next biggest category is leisure and sports, which accounts for 5.18 hours of the average American's day. The average American spends 2.73 hours of this time watching TV.
- Next up is work and work-related activities, which averages 3.5 hours a day.
- Household activities (preparing food, cutting the grass, repairing and decorating the home) account for 1.79 hours a day.
- Eating and drinking take up 1.25 hours.[1]

When you look at the Labor Department statistics, you need to look closely to see how much time is spent on "religious and spiritual activities." For the average American, these activities take up less than 10 minutes of the average day. That's less time than we spend on just about anything else covered by the statistics except for one. For example, the average American spends even less daily time on "household management" (paying bills, balancing the checkbook, and the like) than on spiritual concerns.

People fill their days with work, sleep and other activities. It's no wonder that finding time to love God and to serve our neighbors is such a challenge. It has been a challenge for a long, long time, as Jesus explained when He described His own difficulties finding people who would heed His call and further His mission:

> The harvest is plentiful, but the laborers are few; pray therefore the Lord of the harvest to send out laborers into his harvest (Luke 10:2).

Jesus was able to find 70 people who were willing to serve, and He sent them out two by two to spread His message and heal the sick. But how many people do you think had heard Jesus' teaching in public? Thousands? Tens of thousands? Why did so few heed His call to labor for Christ's eternal harvest? Perhaps they looked at their sundials or their water clocks and decided, "No, I just don't have the time to serve God today."

Things haven't changed much since the time of Jesus. The laborers remain few. Many millions of people call themselves Christians, and many of them attend church. Still, most of the church's work is carried out by a small minority of devoted members. Then as now, too many people are sitting around or they are busy doing things that don't connect to God's work in the world.

Less Can Be More

Most people I know are very busy. At least that's the way it seems whenever I ask them how they're doing. They tell me that work is more demanding. Home life is hectic. Everything is crazy.

The surprising thing is that for most of us, the stress and busyness we complain about are largely self-imposed. Many of us seem to believe that we'll be happier in life if we merely move faster and cram more hustle and bustle into every waking moment. We believe more is more.

I have a radical suggestion: Less can be more. Life can be more fulfilling when we're less frantic. We don't feel the need to shoehorn ever more tasks and activities into each minute in order to have a full life. In fact, when we overburden ourselves, we miss out on the fullness of life that's there for us to enjoy and share.

I am grateful for the many people who have served in our church and who devote their time and energy to the cause of Christ through our ministries or through other redemptive activities in the community. But I am also amazed at the number of Christians who say they simply don't have time when it comes to serving the kingdom of heaven.

That's a curious thing. I thought these people had just as much time in a day as anyone else. The fact is that each one of us has all the time we need. It's like the Irish proverb says, "When God created time, He made plenty of it."

Every morning that we wake up, we are given another day of life. We can't earn it. We can't buy more of it. All we can do is use the time we've been given to the best of our abilities.

Making the Most of Our Time

For most of us, it's not that we don't have enough time; it's that we choose to use our time in ways that don't fulfill our deepest goals and longings. It's not a question of time, but of priorities. What are your priorities?

I don't know the details of your life and your daily calendar. I'm not aware of the pressures and challenges that fill your days. I don't know what takes your time. But I promise you this: Nothing is more important than the kingdom of heaven.

Some of you may say, "Well, my children are more important." Others believe that their jobs are more important. They probably wouldn't actually say it like this: "My work is more important than the kingdom of heaven." But that's how many of us live our lives. We give our top priority to work or other things. God and good works get what's left over, which often isn't much.

Christ was meant to be the center of your life. Anything else is insufficient. The best thing you could ever do for your children or for your job is to put Christ and His kingdom at the center of your life.

Why do so many of us let temporary things take the place of eternal things? Why do we squander our time on insignificant things and lose track of the big things in life? Perhaps it's because we're slaves to the ticking (or beeping) clock, the quarterly report, the annual review. We're wrapped so tightly around the axle that we don't have any time left to serve God's kingdom. In time, we forget about our eternal nature and destiny.

Take it from someone who knows it firsthand: your days are numbered. Life is short. We don't know how long we're going to live. We don't know whether we have days or weeks or months or years remaining on this earth. We don't know whether we will live threescore and ten, or a century or more.

The only thing we know is this: Time is finite, and our days in this world are limited; but we actually have all the time we need to do what we need to do. We don't need more hours in the day. We need to be better stewards of each and every day we have.

How are you going to use the next moment? What do you hope to accomplish tomorrow? If you are fortunate enough to live five more years, how will you make use of this wonderful gift of time?

Whatever you do, I hope you don't tell me, "You know, someday, if I ever have the time, I would like to devote myself more to God's service." Don't dream of doing it someday. Do it today. Do it now.

JIM DIXON

Reflection Questions

1. Complete the following sentence with as many items as you can think of: "If I ever got the time, I would . . ."

2. Grab some kind of calendar that lists the hours and days of a week. Fill in the calendar with where your time goes in a typical week.

    - What observations can you make about the use of your time?
    - What surprised you?
    - What concerns you?
    - What needs to change?

3. Do the priorities that God has for your life show up in your calendar? If not, how will you incorporate them into your regular schedule?

4. What is one activity in your calendar that needs to decrease or go away? What is one activity that needs to increase or be included? When will you implement those changes?

Note

1. "American Time Use Survey," United States Department of Labor, Bureau of Labor Statistics, 2011 Data. http://www.bls.gov/tus/charts/leisure.htm.

8

When Will You Ever Have Enough?

What is it that makes us truly human? For seventeenth-century philosopher René Descartes, the answer was clear:

I think, therefore I am.

Three centuries later, someone updated Descartes's motto for modern times. Here's the new version:

I shop, therefore I am.

You may think the updated motto is funny, or you may think it is sad. Either way, it captures the feeling that today some people place a very high value on their stuff. Finding the appropriate approach toward material goods has been a challenge for at least 20 centuries, as Jesus demonstrated when He shared the parable of the rich man and his barns with a large group of people who were following Him and listening to what He said.

One of the men in the audience asked Jesus to settle a family inheritance issue. Jesus wisely opted out of getting in the middle of this squabble. Instead, He offered this lesson:

> And he said to them, "Take heed, and beware of all covetousness; for a man's life does not consist in the abundance of his possessions."
>
> And he told them a parable, saying, "The land of a rich man brought forth plentifully; and he thought to himself, 'What shall I do, for I have nowhere to store my crops?' And he said, 'I will do this: I will pull down my barns, and build larger ones; and there I will store all my grain and my goods. And I will say to my soul, Soul, you have ample goods laid up for many years; take your ease, eat, drink, be merry.'
>
> But God said to him, 'Fool! This night your soul is required of you; and the things you have prepared, whose will they be?' So is he who lays up treasure for himself, and is not rich toward God."
>
> And he said to his disciples, "Therefore I tell you, do not be anxious about your life, what you shall eat, nor about your body, what you shall put on" (Luke 12:15-22).

Some of us are thinking, *Why did Jesus get so angry at this man? After all, he appears to be a good businessman!*

Jesus may sound a bit harsh, calling the rich man a fool. Jesus didn't typically label people like this. But in this case it was clear: Anyone who believes that life consists of having lots of stuff is mistaken. In fact, the rich man made one of the three classic mistakes of people who live to shop, consume and own. They mistake their stuff for their life.

Is Life Really More Than Stuff?

Economically, it has been a tough few years for Americans and other people around the globe when it comes to wealth. Millions of people have lost their jobs and their homes. Millions more have seen value leaking out of their retirement savings.

They say that every cloud has a silver lining. If I were forced to find a silver lining in the current global recession, it would be this: Many people have been forced to take a fresh look at what they really value.

Before the recession, many Americans equated life with more and more stuff, much of it purchased on credit. Now, many of us are being forced to make do with less and find joy and happiness in other, non-monetary aspects of life. It has been a painful transition, but it has helped some of us get a new perspective on the words of Jesus from the Luke 12 passage above: "Take heed, and beware of all covetousness; for a man's life does not consist in the abundance of his possessions."

Jesus doesn't want us to confuse our sense of our true value in life with the amount of stuff we accumulate. If you say you agree with this, let me give you an easy test.

Suppose God told you to sell your big car and get something a little smaller. Hold on a minute. I'm not saying that's what God wants you to do. That's between you and God, who often requires different things from each and every one of us. I am merely using it as an example for this test.

If God told you to do this, how would you feel about it? Would driving something smaller and cheaper affect the way you feel about yourself? As you get into that more humble car, turn the key and drive to the places you normally drive to, would you feel different about yourself? As you see your friends—and perhaps more importantly, as they see you in your new car—do you feel uncomfortable, vulnerable or even ashamed?

Try these additional tests on for size. Suppose you transitioned in your wardrobe to less expensive and more humble clothing. Would you be able to be "you," or would you feel hampered by your clothes? Would you feel different about yourself as you went around in clothes that were less expensive?

Or suppose you felt that you were suddenly inspired to sell your big home and move into a smaller house that is more affordable and more humble. How would that make you feel about your self-worth? How would that make you feel about your sense of success? How would that make you feel about yourself and the way you value yourself and portray yourself to others?

See what I mean? Most of us are impacted by our possessions much more than we sometimes think. It's not surprising.

It's part of what happens when we live in a culture that is driven by materialism.

When Enough Is Not Enough

Years ago, a man named Steven Berglas wrote a controversial book called *The Success Syndrome*. In the book, Berglas wrote about people who were very successful, people who had made mega-millions, people who had enjoyed success after success after success. One of these über-successful people was named Rick Cholet.

Once upon a time, Rick Cholet was a mega-millionaire. He had built numerous successful businesses, taking them from humble beginnings to corporate greatness. The money just kept on rolling in. That's why everyone was so surprised when on March 18, 1991, Rick Cholet went into the garage of his beautiful New Hampshire home, made sure all the doors were closed, got into his BMW, started the engine and asphyxiated himself.

He left a suicide note that said, "Please forgive me, but I can't take the pain of living anymore."

Berglas wrote that the problem with Rick Cholet was something called "encore anxiety." Encore anxiety often afflicts people who have enjoyed success after success after success. After a while, they don't know what they will do the next time they have an opportunity. Will they be able to repeat their success, or will they finally meet with failure?

I don't really know any details about Rick Cholet's death, but I can say this: While some people struggle with encore anxiety, many of the rest of us suffer other kinds of anxieties when it comes to our wealth and possessions. For many of us, this anxiety goes to the core of our being where it bothers us with questions like these:

- *Do I have enough money?*
- *Am I earning enough?*
- *Have I saved enough to pay for the kids' college and have something left over for retirement?*

In time, these questions can evolve and change until we are asking things like this:

- *I wonder what my friends and neighbors think of me driving around in this five-year-old car. Shouldn't I have something newer?*
- *Am I a bad father or mother if I can't provide all these things for my family?*
- *Am I worth anything if I earn so little?*

Some people become overwhelmed by the pressures of earning money and consuming and possessing. When all of this becomes too much for them to take, they break down. That's the downside to being in a wealthy, materialistic culture. There's an emptiness that can overtake people trying to make it in our materialistic world.

You can build your life upon solid foundations designed by our Creator.

Or you can build your life around stuff; but sooner or later, when you base your sense of personal value on your bank accounts or your possessions, all that stuff ultimately proves how empty and vacuous materialism is. Many of us are dealing with this core anxiety every day, but we don't realize it.

Do you experience anxiety in your soul because of money or possessions? Whether your anxiety comes from having too much, too little or something in between, the words of Jesus show you what needs to be done: "Take heed, and beware of all covetousness; for a man's life does not consist in the abundance of his possessions" (Luke 12:15).

Purse vs. Purpose

The rich man in Jesus' parable valued his stuff over the real things in life. Another problem that afflicts people who struggle with materialism is that we can easily slip into serving money more than we serve God. Jesus described these people in the parable: "he who lays up treasure for himself, and is not rich toward God" (v. 21).

Let me ask you a question: Are you rich? I can remember the discomfort this generated when I asked our congregation this question during my sermon on materialism.

Most people answer by saying, "I'm not rich. After all, Joe Blow down the street lives in a much bigger house than I do. And then there's John Doe with his country club membership and fancy cars. Compared to them, I'm not rich!"

I guess that's one way of answering the question. It's always easy to look around America and find someone who has more than you. But what if we answered the question another way? Suppose we looked at everyone in the world and compared their wealth to ours.

Here's what a United Nations task force report concluded. In today's world, there are three billion people making less than $2 a day. That's nearly one-half of the world's population. Among those three billion people, half of them are making less than $1 a day.[1] That's 1.5 billion earning a dollar a day.

In my home county of Douglas County, just south of Denver, many households earn $250,000 a year. That means they're making about a thousand dollars a day (that's for each working day). What if you are only making $25,000 a year? In the U.S., an annual income of $25,700 is defined as the poverty level for a family of five (according to 2009 government figures). But that impoverishment is still 100 times more than many people earn.

Maybe you're thinking, *A dollar goes further in other places than it does in the U.S.* Tell that to the billions of God's children who live on this earth without the basic needs of life: enough to eat every day, safe water, decent plumbing, basic medical care, education, transportation.

So, I have good news for you. You are rich! Let me be the first to congratulate you. And by the way, now that you have acknowledged your richness, see what Paul says about you in this passage from his first letter to Timothy:

> There is great gain in godliness with contentment; for we brought nothing into the world, and we cannot take

> anything out of the world; but if we have food and clothing, with these we shall be content. But those who desire to be rich fall into temptation, into a snare, into many senseless and hurtful desires that plunge men into ruin and destruction. For the love of money is the root of all evils; it is through this craving that some have wandered away from the faith and pierced their hearts with many pangs (1 Tim. 6:6-10).

One of the problems with being rich is that we get confused about the relationship between purse and purpose. In our confusion, we focus on stuff and self. It's like what Jesus said about the rich man and his barns. The man is so successful that he has to tear down his old barns and build new barns to hold his massive wealth. He's pretty content with himself. He's going to kick back with a beer and some fun entertainment.

But God crashes the party with an announcement for this fool. He who has much should do much. The rich man was supposed to use his purse for God's purposes, not for his own selfish gain and comfort. Beware of the man "who lays up treasure for himself, and is not rich toward God" (Luke 12:21). Paul tells Timothy how to handle such people:

> As for the rich in this world, charge them not to be haughty, nor to set their hopes on uncertain riches but on God who richly furnishes us with everything to enjoy. They are to do good, to be rich in good deeds, liberal and generous, thus laying up for themselves a good

foundation for the future, so that they may take hold of the life which is life indeed (1 Tim. 6:17-19).

Matching Your Purse with Purpose

So, what does it mean to be haughty?

It means to lack humility and to think of yourself as better than everyone else. Many of us in our church family have traveled to Juarez, Mexico, as part of our short-term missions outreach. In Juarez, we've visited impoverished communities—some of them adjacent to large garbage dumps—where thousands upon thousands of people live in simple lean-to structures or empty cardboard boxes. If you look at these people and think you are better than they are, you are haughty. You're a fool. And if after spending a day with the mission group you return to your nice resort hotel, and as you are lying on your bed you think that somehow you're better than the impoverished people you were around all day, you are haughty. You're a fool.

Then what does it mean to match purse with purpose? Let me give you an example of a rich man who did exactly that.

By the world's standards, R. G. LeTourneau was an incredibly successful man. He built an earth-moving machinery company that manufactured the earth-moving equipment that gave us the Alaskan highway. It was LeTourneau's earth-moving equipment that stormed the beaches at Normandy. It was LeTourneau's earth-moving equipment that removed 5,000 acres of swampland to build the Kennedy International Airport.

LeTourneau grew very, very rich, and he loved Jesus Christ, so he knew he had to tie his purse to his purpose. He couldn't just be rich toward himself; he had to be rich toward God. So he lived his life in a very special way as he began to give it all away. Starting as a young man, when he didn't have much money, he tithed, giving away 10 percent of his income for godly purposes. But as his wealth multiplied, LeTourneau decided 10 percent wasn't enough, so he increased the amount he gave away every year to 20 percent, then 30 percent, 40 percent, and 50 percent of his income.

He wasn't done. As the wealth continued to flow in, he made sure it continued to flow out to worthy causes, including Christian schools and conference centers that bear his name, giving away 60 percent, 70 percent, 80 percent, and then 90 percent of his income. By his later years, that wasn't enough; so he gave away 100 percent of what he earned.

LeTourneau died in 1969, but before his death, people repeatedly asked him about his aggressive charitable giving. He was always pleased to explain that it started with God.

"When you know Him, you'll love Him; and when you love Him, you'll serve Him, and find the greatest happiness in doing so that you'll ever know," he said. "It's not how much of my money I give to God, but how much of His money I keep for myself."

You may not have LeTourneau's wealth, but Jesus wants you to share his commitment. I don't care how much money you think you have or don't have. Unless you handle your resources in ways that are rich toward God, you are a fool. Give it away!

A MATTER OF TRUST

R. G. LeTourneau trusted God with his finances. What about you? If you're an American, you use dollar bills that say, "In God We Trust." But do we really trust God when it comes to money? I'm not so sure.

Which brings us to the third lesson about money from Jesus' parable. First, we learned that we mistake stuff for life. Second, we know that we serve money more than we serve God. The third problem many of us have with money is that we trust it more than we trust God and His promises about life.

How can we tell if we are guilty of having misplaced our trust? How do we know if we are giving ourselves to material things rather than to spiritual things? One way to tell is to do the anxiety test. Are you anxious about money, possessions or your financial future? If so, you are directly disobeying the command of Jesus, who tells us not to be anxious about these things.

After Jesus told the crowd the parable about the rich man and his barns, He followed up with a mini-sermon on money:

> Therefore I tell you, do not be anxious about your life, what you shall eat, nor about your body, what you shall put on. For life is more than food, and the body more than clothing.
>
> Consider the ravens: they neither sow nor reap, they have neither storehouse nor barn, and yet God feeds them. Of how much more value are you than the birds! And which of you by being anxious can

> add a cubit to his span of life? If then you are not able to do as small a thing as that, why are you anxious about the rest?
>
> Consider the lilies, how they grow; they neither toil nor spin; yet I tell you, even Solomon in all his glory was not arrayed like one of these. But if God so clothes the grass which is alive in the field today and tomorrow is thrown into the oven, how much more will he clothe you, O men of little faith!
>
> And do not seek what you are to eat and what you are to drink, nor be of anxious mind. For all the nations of the world seek these things; and your Father knows that you need them. Instead, seek his kingdom, and these things shall be yours as well (Luke 12:22-31).

Tragedies always test our trust. That was especially true for Americans on September 11, 2001, the day of the attacks on the World Trade Center and the Pentagon. My wife and I were out of the country on 9/11. It felt terrible to be watching this tragedy unfold on a little TV on the other side of the world.

Losses were great on that day, but one particular loss symbolized the transience of material wealth. High up in one of the World Trade Center towers were the offices of a company that traded in precious metals. On that day, 12 tons of the company's gold melted down and mixed with the rubble. But were the firemen and police at the site seeking gold? No, they were looking first for signs of life among the smoldering remains. Goal number two was to recover the remains of the deceased.

The men and women working at Ground Zero didn't have time to think about gold.

Tragedy can do that. Have you ever gone through a horrible experience that suddenly gives everything in life a different value? Suddenly you see things more clearly. You understand value in a clear way. Jesus wants us to have that kind of clarity when we look at our stuff. Hopefully, we will see that our stuff is just stuff, and we won't need a tragedy to cause a paradigm shift.

A Very Good Year

In 1932, a man named George Beverly Shea was offered a lucrative contract to perform on the radio for a huge national audience. This singer turned down the lucrative contract because he wanted to do something more important with his talent: sing for evangelistic meetings and rallies in the Chicago area.

Shea probably thought his career choice would lead to a life of obscurity. Perhaps that's why he wrote a song titled "I'd Rather Have Jesus," which featured these words:

I'd rather have Jesus than silver or gold.
I'd rather be his than have riches untold.
I'd rather have Jesus than houses or land,
I'd rather be led by his nail-pierced hands
Than to be a king of a vast domain,
or to be held in sin's dread sway
I'd rather have Jesus than anything
the world affords today.

Something unexpected happened to this talented singer who wanted to sing for God. He agreed to sing at the evangelistic rallies featuring a young preacher named Billy Graham. That was the end of obscurity. *The Guinness Book of Records* says Shea holds the world record for singing in person to the most people ever, with an estimated cumulative live audience of 220 million.

What would have happened if George Beverly Shea had based his career decision on the best available financial and professional calculations? If that had been his goal, Shea probably would have chosen the lucrative radio contract. Instead, he trusted God and went out on a limb. Today, we celebrate that decision.

Getting Radical

Are there decisions you face where there's tension between what you want to do and what you feel makes the best financial sense? It happens all the time. That's why mega-church pastor David Platt wrote his book *Radical: Taking Back Your Faith from the American Dream*.

Platt was serving a large congregation in Alabama when he realized he was "on a collision course with the American church culture where success is defined by bigger crowds, bigger budgets, and bigger buildings." Platt says he realized something important: "Jesus actually spurned the things my church culture said were most important."[2]

I guess even churches can get it wrong about where to place their trust.

So what can we do to put Jesus' principles into practice in our lives? One way to do it is to make some radical changes. If that scares you, you can start in a gradual manner.

How much of your annual income are you giving away right now? One way to get radical gradually is to increase your giving by 1 percent, or 5 percent. Surveys show that many Christians donate only about 2 percent of their income. If that figure fits you, how about taking a radical/gradual approach by giving away 3 percent or 4 percent of your income? That's still less than the 10 percent many leaders recommend, and far less than the 100 percent LeTourneau gave away late in his life.

I'll leave it to you to determine the practical steps that will work for you. But Jesus' teaching is clear. Our behavior reveals what we value, and one way to change things when our values are mixed up is to behave differently.

It's like Jesus told His disciples:

> The kingdom of heaven is like treasure hidden in a field, which a man found and covered up; then in his joy he goes and sells all that he has and buys that field (Matt. 13:44).

Reflection Questions

1. How would you describe your general attitude and feelings about money?

2. Which of the six lessons on finances is the most difficult for you to embrace? Why?

3. What kind of daily practice would help you to remember that God really does own it all?

4. What would it look like for you to become a cheerful and extravagant giver of your finances?

5. If possible, look back at the last 6-12 months of your budget or checkbook register.

    - What strikes you concerning how you have used your money?
    - Does the use of your money reflect the six lessons on finances?
    - What changes or adjustments do you need to make to help you be a good and faithful steward of the finances God has entrusted to you?

Notes

1. "Globalization," Report from the United Nations. www.un.org/cyberschoolbus/briefing/globalization/globalization.pdf.
2. David Platt, *Radical: Taking Back Your Faith from the American Dream* (Colorado Springs, CO: Multnomah Books, 2010).

9

Does Your Faith Influence Your Finances?

Over the centuries, Christian leaders have developed various "tests" to see how committed Christians are. After all, anyone can say they love God, but how can they prove it?

Some leaders have said that the true test of commitment is regular church attendance and service. Others focus on evangelism, saying that if you don't share your faith with others your faith must not really mean that much to you. Still others want to know how many Bible verses you have memorized, or how much you pray and fast, or what your views on sexuality or politics are.

As for me, I have my own surefire way of assessing how committed someone is. My test is a simple one: What do you do with your money?

"Oh, no!" I can hear some of you say. "Here comes another preacher going after my money." This anxiety is understandable. Too many well-known Christian leaders have been exposed by the media or the government for turning ministries into cash cows that provide mansions, cars, jets, jewelry (and, in one high-profile case, an air-conditioned dog house).

These excesses show that money's temptations can become too powerful to resist. That's why I want to focus on six key lessons on money found in the New Testament. If you want to follow Christ in all aspects of life, including the financial aspect, come along on the journey. I think you'll be surprised by what you find.

Lesson 1: Help Others in Tough Times

It has been difficult to live through America's latest economic recession, but this isn't the first time things have been tough. Back in the earliest years of the Christian movement, Jews in Jerusalem who had accepted Jesus were ostracized from their families and fired from their jobs. How would these Jewish followers of Jesus survive? Paul had a radical idea: Believers throughout the world would donate some of their wealth to help these persecuted brothers and sisters.

Paul was the leading fund-raiser for the Jerusalem Collection. Offerings were collected every Sunday in churches and fellowships in order to raise funds for Jerusalem's Jews. These offerings were called *allogia*, which means "an extra offering" or a "secondary offering." That means these donations were over and above the normal offerings that were given to the local church.

This historical episode provides our first New Testament lesson on finances: Christians give to help others. They have done so since the earliest days of the Christian faith, and they do so today, with believers who have surplus resources helping those who have less.

This kind of charitable giving is a good thing. In fact, Jesus says it may be the best thing: "It is more blessed to give than to receive" (Acts 20:35). Our world doesn't seem to believe that. Most people seem to believe that it's more blessed to receive than to give. Jesus disagrees, using the word *makarizo,* which means "happy." It's through giving that we become happy, Jesus tells us, not through receiving.

In Paul's day the Jews in Jerusalem needed help. Today, people down the street and around the globe need our help. Those of us who have enough should do our part, just as believers have done from the beginning.

Lesson 2: Give Generously

In explaining the Jerusalem Collection in his second letter to the Christians at Corinth, Paul made his case:

> Now it is superfluous for me to write to you about the offering for the saints, for I know your readiness, of

> which I boast about you to the people of Macedo'nia, saying that Acha'ia has been ready since last year; and your zeal has stirred up most of them. But I am sending the brethren so that our boasting about you may not prove vain in this case, so that you may be ready, as I said you would be; lest if some Macedo'nians come with me and find that you are not ready, we be humiliated—to say nothing of you—for being so confident. So I thought it necessary to urge the brethren to go on to you before me, and arrange in advance for this gift you have promised, so that it may be ready not as an exaction but as a willing gift. The point is this: he who sows sparingly will also reap sparingly, and he who sows bountifully will also reap bountifully (2 Cor. 9:1-6).

Here Paul provides our second financial lesson of the day: Sow bountifully. In other words, give generously. Don't merely toss a few coins in the collection plate and call it quits. Dig down deeply and give bountifully.

What does "bountifully" mean? The New Testament doesn't define an amount that believers should give. Many Christians throughout history have relied on the Old Testament practice of tithing, which is spelled out in Deuteronomy and requires that people give God 10 percent of their income. I don't consider giving one-tenth of your income to be giving bountifully. It's more the baseline norm that God expects. In reality, fewer than 5 percent of Christians today donate a full tithe. Many give only 1 or 2 percent of their income. Some give nothing.

There are two reasons God wants you to give generously. One reason concerns the recipients. The more you give, the more the recipients will be helped. The second reason concerns the giver. The more you give, the more you will reap.

Some evangelists have twisted Paul's words about reaping to suggest that if you give $1,000, God will give you $1,000 back in return, or maybe even $10,000. But the New Testament doesn't say that. We should give to give, not to receive. And if we give bountifully, we can trust God that we will reap bountifully, even if we don't get money back in the process.

God wants you to know that you're on this earth for only a brief time, and the time you are here is your opportunity to increase His kingdom and to sow bountifully. Or as writer Maya Angelou puts it, "I have found that among its other benefits, giving liberates the soul of the giver."

Lesson 3: Give Cheerfully

If you've ever read O. Henry's classic story "The Gift of the Magi," you know it explores the Christmas crisis faced by Jim and Della, a young married couple with little money for Christmas presents. As O. Henry states, the couple had one dollar and 87 cents, and 60 cents of it was in pennies: "Pennies saved one and two at a time by bulldozing the grocer and the vegetable man and the butcher until one's cheeks burned with the silent imputation of parsimony that such close dealing implied. Three times Della counted it. One dollar and eighty-seven cents. And the next day would be Christmas."

In the story, Jim and Della both decide to sacrifice something important in order to give a gift to the other. O. Henry ends the story with an emotional plot twist that makes their sacrifices even more meaningful and touching. Jim and Della don't have much, but they know what it means to give, and give cheerfully.

God wants us to give in a similar manner. He wants us to be so committed to giving that we don't hold back because of the sacrifice involved. Paul explained this concept in his letter to the Corinthians:

> Each one must do as he has made up his mind, not reluctantly or under compulsion, for God loves a cheerful giver. And God is able to provide you with every blessing in abundance, so that you may always have enough of everything and may provide in abundance for every good work.
>
> As it is written, "He scatters abroad, he gives to the poor; his righteousness endures for ever."
>
> He who supplies seed to the sower and bread for food will supply and multiply your resources and increase the harvest of your righteousness. You will be enriched in every way for great generosity, which through us will produce thanksgiving to God; for the rendering of this service not only supplies the wants of the saints but also overflows in many thanksgivings to God. Under the test of this service, you will glorify God by your obedience in acknowledging the gospel of Christ, and

> by the generosity of your contribution for them and for all others; while they long for you and pray for you, because of the surpassing grace of God in you. Thanks be to God for his inexpressible gift! (2 Cor. 9:7-15).

The word for cheerful in this passage is the word *hileros*, the Greek word from which we get the English word "hilarious." In other words, Paul is telling us, "God loves a hilarious giver." Giving is a good thing to do, but if you give with reservations, resentment or regret, you are missing out on the big picture.

Lesson 4: God Owns Everything

The Yakama Indian Nation has a long and proud history that continues with the Yakama Indians who live on a reservation in the state of Washington. After the year 2000, the Yakamas found themselves in a legal dispute with the U.S. government over the subject of who owns the rain.

There's a federal agency called the Bonneville Power Administration that regulates and disburses the energy from the federal dams along the Columbia River. The problem is that a drought had reduced rain in that region, which led the Yakamas to perform two rain dances. After the rain dances, rain in the region increased slightly. So the Yakamas billed the federal government $32,000. The feds declined to pay, saying, "We don't pay God for rain."

It raises an interesting question: Who owns the rain? Similarly complex questions of ownership arise in many scenarios.

For example, if you own property in Colorado, you own the land but not the mineral rights for any riches that are found buried on your property.

The Bible takes a radically different approach than we do. God owns the rain and the minerals, not the government, not the Yakamas, not the mineral companies. King David said as much in Psalm 24:1-2 (a passage that Paul quotes in 1 Corinthians 10:26):

> The earth is the LORD's and the fullness thereof, the world and those who dwell therein; for he has founded it upon the seas, and established it upon the rivers.

We live in a world where it is common to think of things as "mine, all mine!" After all, it's our name—not God's name—in the "owner" blank of our auto title, our house mortgage and our monthly credit card bills. But in truth, it's *all* His. Everything belongs to God. When you drive "your" car today or walk into "your" home or apartment, you need to remember that everything belongs to God.

The Early Church understood this concept, as we can see from ancient baptismal rituals. As believers were taken under the water in full immersion baptism, they used the word *doulos* to describe themselves as slaves. Even their lives were not their own. God owns everything, including us.

Many believers can theoretically accept this concept that God owns everything, but some want an exception for their money and possessions. When they are baptized, they want to protect their wallets and purses from the water and from God's ownership. "God owns everything *but* my financial assets." That's not the way it's supposed to be. Everything is God's. He is the owner. We'll never be good stewards with regard to our money unless we acknowledge that and understand that.

Lesson 5: God Wants Us to Be Good Stewards of His Stuff

If you've ever read a book or heard a sermon about stewardship, you've probably come across Jesus' parable of the talents, which is found in Matthew 25:

> For it will be as when a man going on a journey called his servants and entrusted to them his property; to one he gave five talents, to another two, to another one, to each according to his ability. Then he went away. He who had received the five talents went at once and traded with them; and he made five talents more. So also, he who had the two talents made two talents more. But he who had received the one talent went and dug in the ground and hid his master's money.
>
> Now after a long time the master of those servants came and settled accounts with them. And he who had received the five talents came forward, bringing five talents more, saying, "Master, you delivered to me five talents; here I have made five talents more."
>
> His master said to him, "Well done, good and faithful servant; you have been faithful over a little, I will set you over much; enter into the joy of your master."

> And he also who had the two talents came forward, saying, "Master, you delivered to me two talents; here I have made two talents more."
>
> His master said to him, "Well done, good and faithful servant; you have been faithful over a little, I will set you over much; enter into the joy of your master."
>
> He also who had received the one talent came forward, saying, "Master, I knew you to be a hard man, reaping where you did not sow, and gathering where you did not winnow; so I was afraid, and I went and hid your talent in the ground. Here you have what is yours."
>
> But his master answered him, "You wicked and slothful servant! You knew that I reap where I have not sowed, and gather where I have not winnowed? Then you ought to have invested my money with the bankers, and at my coming I should have received what was my own with interest.
>
> "So take the talent from him, and give it to him who has the ten talents. For to every one who has will more be given, and he will have abundance; but from him who has not, even what he has will be taken away. And cast the worthless servant into the outer darkness; there men will weep and gnash their teeth" (vv. 14-30).

This is a fascinating parable that illustrates an important principle: God seeks productivity from His stewards. The master entrusts his property to his servants to take care of it. We saw in Lesson 4 that everything is God's property. Here in Lesson 5 the emphasis is not ownership but productivity.

You are to grow the goods that have been entrusted to you by the Master. Everything God has placed in your care needs to increase and flourish under your stewardship. God wants you to be productive.

Some people mistakenly interpret the Parable of the Talents, turning it into a me-centered story about personal transformation and reaching our full potential. This egocentric interpretation says that God has given us talents and abilities and aptitudes and giftedness, and that we are to cultivate them and become all that we can be. But that's not really the point Jesus is making in the Parable of the Talents. This egocentric interpretation sounds more like what you hear from Oprah or Dr. Phil. The point of the parable is not about you and me reaching our potential; it's about the kingdom of heaven.

We have been invited to be a part of the kingdom of heaven that Jesus announced. When we stand before Christ at the final judgment, He won't be inquiring about whether we are fulfilled and content. He will want to know if we have used our lives and resources to help build the heavenly kingdom.

Lesson 6: God Wants Us to Give Extravagantly

Investing in the kingdom of heaven is not the same as investing in a 401k retirement plan. A well-funded 401k may cover the costs of your retirement, which could last a few decades. An investment in the kingdom of God lasts forever. That's why we should devote our very best to God's kingdom, as we see in this episode from the New Testament:

> Now when Jesus was at Bethany in the house of Simon the leper, a woman came up to him with an alabaster flask of very expensive ointment, and she poured it on his head, as he sat at table.
>
> But when the disciples saw it, they were indignant, saying, "Why this waste? For this ointment might have been sold for a large sum, and given to the poor."
>
> But Jesus, aware of this, said to them, "Why do you trouble the woman? For she has done a beautiful thing to me. For you always have the poor with you, but you will not always have me. In pouring this ointment on my body she has done it to prepare me for burial. Truly, I say to you, wherever this gospel is preached in the whole world, what she has done will be told in memory of her" (Matt. 26:6-13).

Matthew doesn't even tell us the woman's name (John tells us she is Mary of Bethany, the same woman who sat at Jesus' feet while her sister Martha was so busy). Matthew wasn't trying to hide Mary's identity. It's just that he wanted to emphasize her act of extravagant love. In anointing Jesus with the perfume, Mary expressed her love of Jesus so powerfully that Jesus said the story of her act would be told again and again throughout the world.

How Radical Is Your Commitment to Christ?

When you put it all together, the six lessons on finances we have covered in this chapter paint a picture of what it means to be a true disciple of Jesus. The picture portrays believers who will cheerfully and gratefully lavish money, time and energy on serving God, caring for others and helping to build the kingdom of God.

Is this the picture of what you see when you look into a mirror? If not, start building this chapter's lessons into your life so that you can allow God to own you, along with all "your" stuff.

Reflection Questions

1. What would you say is your greatest fear in this life? What fuels that deep-seated anxiety?

2. Think for a moment about the events and situations in life that cause you to experience ongoing anxiety or fear. What are some common denominators to your anxieties? Can you identify any recurring patterns or themes?

3. Make a list of all the things in life you cannot control or change. How many of those items or situations do you find yourself worrying over? What would it look like for you to cast those anxieties on Christ (see 1 Pet. 5:6-7)?

4. How could you have a more open-handed acceptance of whatever God has in store for your life? How do you think such a surrendered and submitted heart would affect the level of your anxiety?

Take a few hours and head to a park or open space. Take some time to observe the birds of the air and the lilies of the field. Record what you learned.

10

What Are You Afraid Of?

They called Gunther Gebel-Williams "The Greatest Wild Animal Trainer of All Time!" He performed for more than 200 million people between 1968 and 1990 with the Ringling Bros. and Barnum & Bailey Circus.

Taming lions would be a tough job on a good night. I can't imagine what it was like the night the lights suddenly went out in the big tent in the middle of a show. Gebel-Williams was standing in the center of a circle of 20 Bengal tigers with his trainer's chair in one hand and his whip in the other. He was doing his standard tricks with the animals and basking in the audience's applause when an electrical short caused the tent to go completely dark. He couldn't see his hand in front of his face, let alone the big animals that encircled him.

Tigers are the largest members of the cat family, with females weighing up to 450 pounds and the males reaching weights of 900 pounds. Each animal can jump up to 30 feet through the air. With one swipe of its powerful foreleg, the Bengal tiger can take a human life in an instant. They can also see in the dark!

Gebel-Williams knew the 20 tigers could see him. He also knew one other important fact. The tigers were not aware that he could not see them. So he did what any veteran lion tamer would do. He faked it, moving around and around the circle of animals until the lights came back on minutes later.

Do you ever feel like you're in the dark while surrounded by life: kids at home, bosses at work, financial worries that invade your nights, personal anxieties that trouble your days, and other challenges and tormentors that seemingly encircle you?

Have you ever stopped to ask yourself, *What am I so afraid of?* Have you ever considered the possibility of living your life without fear? Whether you're a professional worrywart or just an average anxious person, I want to tell you some good news that can change your life.

An Antidote for the Acid of Anxiety

We live in an anxious age, and over the last few years, economic anxieties have amped up the anxieties of individuals and nations around the globe. For individuals, it's unemployment, lack of health insurance and falling housing prices that have caused the most anxiety. For nations, it's been instability in stock markets, runaway spending, decreased income from taxes, and fears of market crashes that have increased anxiety for all of us.

Jesus understands our anxieties, but He doesn't want us to be consumed by them, as He explained in His Sermon on the Mount:

> Therefore I tell you, do not be anxious about your life, what you shall eat or what you shall drink, nor about your body, what you shall put on. Is not life more than food, and the body more than clothing? Look at the birds of the air: they neither sow nor reap nor gather into barns, and yet your Heavenly Father feeds them. Are you not of more value than they? And which of you by being anxious can add one cubit to his span of life?
>
> And why are you anxious about clothing. Consider the lilies of the field, how they grow; they neither toil nor spin; yet I tell you, even Solomon in all of his glory was not arrayed like one of these. But if God so clothes the grass of the field, which today is alive and tomorrow is thrown in the oven, will he not much more clothe you, O men of little faith? Therefore do not be anxious, saying, "What shall we eat?" or "What shall we drink?" or "What shall we wear?" For the gentiles seek all these things; and your heavenly Father knows that you need them all. But seek first his kingdom and his righteousness, and all these things shall be yours as well. Therefore do not be anxious about tomorrow, for tomorrow will be anxious for itself. Let the day's own trouble be sufficient for the day (Matt. 6:25-34).

This is the will of Christ for His people: that we would learn to live without worry. The Bible uses many ancient words that are translated in our Bibles as "fear." One of these words is the word *phobos*, the Greek word from which we get the word "phobic." This is one of the Bible's primary words for fear. But there is another Greek word, *merimna,* which describes anxiety and worry. This is what Jesus is addressing in the Matthew 6 passage.

Can you picture a life without worry and anxiety? It may be hard to picture this if you feel that you are standing in the dark surrounded by dozens of tigers. But no matter what anxieties you face, Jesus wants you to trust Him rather than become fearful over things you can't really change. Let's apply Jesus' message to a few of the most common fears that plague us.

1. The Fear of Failure

Once upon a time there was a young man named Sparky. By the time he was in his teens, many people already considered him a loser. In middle school, he flunked every single course he took during his eighth-grade year, and he had to repeat the entire year. In high school, he flunked physics, algebra, Latin and English.

He also was a failure athletically. He seldom tried out for any sports, and when he did, he was an embarrassment. During his senior year, he went out for golf, but he only competed in two matches, doing horribly in both. His coach was clear: "Sparky, feel free to try something else."

Sparky also failed at relationships. He had a hard time making friends. While growing up, he was virtually alone. He never had a single date in all of high school.

But this young man who was considered a failure and a loser could do one thing very well. He could draw cartoons and comic strips. In his senior year, he submitted a comic strip to the yearbook committee, but it was rejected. He had failed again; but he kept trying, and sent some of his work to the Walt Disney Corporation, which initially expressed interest before finally wishing him better luck elsewhere. Once again he had come up empty.

After serving in World War II, Sparky moved to Minnesota to work as an art teacher and began doing comic strips for a local newspaper. One of the characters in his strips was named Charlie Brown. In time, Charlie Brown and the other characters in the comic strip would become phenomenally famous. Sparky's comic strip was called "Peanuts." Sparky died in 2000, but "Peanuts" is still published in newspapers around the world. Overall, the Peanuts comic strips, books and other products have generated over $1 billion in sales.

Sparky (whose real name was Charles Schulz) was a Christian; so even when he failed at something, he knew that Christ still loved him. This faith helped him keep trying to succeed in spite of his repeated failures.

What about you? Have you ever failed at something? Have things not gone the way you hoped and, as a result, you are afraid of ever trying anything again? If so, I beg you: Don't let fear caused by failures of the past darken your hope for the future.

Fear of Failure in the Church

God wants all of us to serve His Church, but I know many people who let fear stop them. They are afraid their voices are not good enough to sing in the choir or help with worship. They're afraid they don't know enough theology to teach Sunday School class. They are afraid their hands are too cold to serve as greeters on Sunday mornings.

Jesus addressed this kind of fear in a parable about a nobleman who was going away on a journey, but before he left he gave some of his money to his servants and asked them to use it wisely during his absence. All of the servants invested the money and made a profit except for one servant, who explained his inaction by telling his master, "I was afraid" (Luke 19:21). Here, the New Testament uses that word *phobos*.

The master judged this servant harshly for giving in to fear. Jesus doesn't want us to shrink back in fear when we have opportunities to serve. He wants us to take risks for the kingdom of God and for the cause of heaven. He wants us to be willing to step out of our comfort zone and take a risk for a higher calling.

Fear of failure keeps people from ministry in the church, but Jesus wants us to serve without fear. The Church of Jesus Christ is only as strong as its members' commitment. Don't let fear stop you from playing your part.

2. The Fear of Rejection

I share my December 10 birthday with poet Emily Dickinson, who was born on December 10, 1830, and lived her whole life in a house in Amherst, Massachusetts. Growing up, she almost never left the house. After her father died when she was 30 years old, she grew even more reclusive, staying indoors for the next 27 years and spending almost every moment in her bedroom on the second floor.

When she died at age 57, people wanted to know what she had been doing with herself all that time. When her family searched her room, they discovered nearly 1,800 poems she had written. Today, many scholars regard her as the greatest female English-speaking poet in world history.

Biographers disagree about many aspects of Dickinson's life, but most attribute her self-imposed isolation to her fear of rejection—a fear that may have begun during her teenage years when she fell in love with a boy who rejected her. The fact that she could love someone so completely, only to be rejected, brought her so much suffering that she resolved to never experience that kind of pain again, and she cut herself off from the world.

Dickinson suffered from a more extreme version of something that many of us deal with: fear of rejection. If you've ever experienced it, rejection can be very painful and very personal. Fear of rejection is certainly understandable, but allowing it to determine what we do is a sin.

Love is risky, yet God calls all of us to love God and love our neighbors. Jesus taught that the Scriptures could be summed up by one word: "love." John's Gospel strongly encourages us that the world will know we are Christians by our love (see John 13:35).

Love is not a concept; it is something that must be expressed through action. That's why we are called to go out into the world as ambassadors of God's selfless love. We are called to love our neighbors, our spouses, our children, our co-workers and everyone else we come into contact with. Jesus even said we are to love our enemies (see Luke 6:35).

There are risks everywhere, but Jesus showed us through His life and death that we should love others unhindered by the fear of rejection, just as He did. Jesus knew He would be rejected. He knew He would die on a cross, but He came to our planet anyway. He chose to love. Now He wants us to do the same: "A new commandment I give to you, that you love" (John 13:34).

Unfortunately, our fear of rejection can cause us to disobey Christ's command to love others as He loved us. It's not easy talking to someone in your neighborhood and trying to befriend him or her. What if he or she doesn't like you? Doesn't want to talk to you? Doesn't want to be your friend? But we can't turn away from life like Emily Dickinson did. Loving others is the call of Jesus for each and every one of us.

3. Fear's Final Frontier

"Houston, we have a problem." For the astronauts on *Apollo 13*, the problems with their malfunctioning space capsule were magnified by the fact that they more than 200,000 miles away from planet Earth. An oxygen tank had exploded, crippling key equipment that controlled their air, water, power and heat. It was 1970, and I remember wondering, *As these brave men hurtle through space, do they struggle with thanatophobia?* It's a big word, signifying one of life's most powerful phobias: the fear of death.

Everyone dies, so perhaps we should say, "Earth, we have a problem!" Many people are afraid of dying. Some fear being dead while others are more afraid of the actual process of dying. For some, there's also fear about what happens after death.

For many of us, the fear of death is like a dim but constant background noise. We may not always notice it, but it's always there. For other people, the fear of death is so pronounced that it negatively impacts their ability to live life or connect with others. These people truly experience full-blown thanatophobia.

I see fear of death impacting Christians in a variety of ways. For example, I think some believers may fill their lives with material goods in order to fight back against and suppress their fears of annihilation. Or perhaps they are fearful of helping people who are sick or dying because contact with such people reminds them of their own mortality.

No matter where you fall on the thanatophobia scale, the human death rate is 100 percent. Each and every one of us is racing toward death. So we should learn to deal with it.

Like the crew on *Apollo 13*, we all have system failures. Our bodies eventually fail us, either in small ways or major ways. Minds can fail, too. Illnesses like Alzheimer's disease can lead to one of the saddest things in human life: the experience of seeing a person you have known and loved for decades forget who you are as his or her brain loses its former abilities.

Jesus knew humans had a thing about death. That's part of why He came into our world:

> Since therefore the children share in flesh and blood, he himself likewise partook of the same nature, that through death he might destroy him who has the power of death, that is, the devil, and deliver all those who through fear of death were subject to lifelong bondage. For surely it is not with angels that he is concerned but with the descendants of Abraham. Therefore he had to be made like his brethren in every respect, so that he might become a merciful and faithful high priest in the service of God, to make expiation for the sins of the people. For because he himself has suffered and been tempted, he is able to help those who are tempted (Heb. 2:14-18).

This fascinating but complex passage tells us that the whole world is in lifelong bondage because of our fear of death. Jesus has come into the world to destroy death and to release the crippling stranglehold death has in our lives.

The resurrection of Christ shows us that for those who follow Christ, death is not the end of life, but merely the transition to everlasting life. We don't know what all this will look like or feel like, but each one of us has an eternal soul that is separated from the body at death and united with God.

If more people believed this, we wouldn't need TV shows like "Crossing Over with Jon Edward." Edward, whose website describes him as "a psychic medium, author and lecturer," hosts a popular cable TV series featuring dramatic reenactments of his efforts to communicate with the souls of the dead. The messages he claims to bring back encourage grieving loved ones who pay $195 or more to attend Edward's public appearances.

Although the Bible condemns mediums, Americans have a long history of fascination with contacting people who have died. One of the most passionate amateur mediums was Thomas Edison, the brilliant and unique man who invented the electric light, the phonograph and motion pictures. In a 1923 interview with *Scientific American* magazine, Edison unveiled a surprise.

"I'm working on a new invention and it's going to be my greatest invention," he said.

"What is it?" the editor asked.

"It's a device that will enable us to communicate with the dead," replied Edison.

He did not know where souls went, but he felt that somehow they were in touch with electric particles that permeated our atmosphere. His plan was to craft a machine that would connect with these particles, enabling him to communicate with the souls of the dead.

I don't know if that sounds like science or science fiction to you, but Edison's passion for "crossing over" to the other side could be traced to the fact that he grieved the loss of his mother. He couldn't bear the pain of that separation and wanted to talk to her beyond the grave.

My mom died a few years ago, so I can understand what Edison was feeling. God blessed my mom with a long life. Her first 94 years were absolutely wonderful, but her final year was pretty hard. Now I miss her. I miss being able to talk to her. On the other hand, I trust that I will be able to be with her in the next life. I don't know how that will happen, but I believe it will.

I am not fearful or anxious about my own death. I know I belong to Jesus Christ and I'm bound for heaven by His grace and mercy. I certainly don't look forward to leaving my wife, Barb, behind. She and I have talked together about death, and I know she feels the same way about leaving me.

Recently, when I had hip surgery, she talked to the surgeon. "Be careful," she told him, "we're joined at the hip." The truth is, it's far deeper than that. We're joined at the heart. We're joined in the soul.

It would be difficult to lose each other and leave behind our kids, our grandkids and all the friends we have known for so many years. We don't want to leave the people who have meant the most to us throughout life. We are sorrowful about death and how it ravages the minds and bodies of loved ones. But we are not afraid. We have trusted God in life, and we will trust Him in death as well.

A Mountaintop Experience

Martin Luther King Jr. gave his final speech on April 3, 1968, the night before he was shot and killed in Memphis. King, who studied theology as a divinity student before becoming a pastor, captured the experience believers have as they anticipate their own deaths:

> Well, I don't know what will happen now. We've got some difficult days ahead. But it really doesn't matter

> with me now, because I've been to the mountaintop. And I don't mind. Like anybody, I would like to live a long life. Longevity has its place. But I'm not concerned about that now. I just want to do God's will. And He's allowed me to go up to the mountain. And I've looked over. And I've seen the Promised Land.[1]

Was King speaking about the promised land of civil rights in America or the promise of eternal life given to all Christians? Perhaps he was referring to both. Either way, I am moved by his openhanded acceptance of whatever it was that God had in store for him, in life or in death.

Perhaps this chapter has stirred long-buried fears that have a powerful impact on you. Are you afraid of failure? Are you afraid of rejection? Are you afraid of death?

Christ doesn't promise freedom from life's problems, but He does offer us an alternative to our fears if we choose to embrace it. God is with us. We do not walk alone. His presence in our lives gives us direction and a redemptive purpose in life. At the end of life, we will walk into the warmth of His eternal embrace.

This assurance should give you comfort and strength as you stand in the dark and stare down the tigers that surround you!

Oswald Chambers, the renowned Scottish minister, teacher and author, said there is one fear to which we should submit:

> The remarkable thing about fearing God is that when you fear God you fear nothing else, whereas if you do not fear God, you fear everything else.[2]

Reflection Questions

1. When was a time in your life when you stood up for someone or took a stand for something? What was that experience like?

2. Look up the following verses of Scripture. What do they say we should be "standoffish" toward?

   - Romans 13:14
   - 1 Corinthians 6:18-20; 10:14
   - 1 Timothy 6:10-11
   - 2 Timothy 2:22-23
   - James 4:6-7

3. Are there any areas of your life where you need to be more standoffish? If so, what are some specific practices you could implement daily to help you avoid evil?

4. How could you more consistently model the love and character of Christ in your interactions with other people? At home? At work?

5. Prayerfully ask God if there is any place or situation where He is asking you to take a stand for your faith in Christ. What would it look like for you to "stand up for Jesus" in these places?

Notes

1. Martin Luther King Jr., "I've Been to the Mountaintop," speech delivered April 3, 1968, at the Mason Temple in Memphis, Tennessee. http://www.afscme.org/union/history/mlk/ive-been-to-the-mountaintop-by-dr-martin-luther-king-jr.
2. Oswald Chambers, *My Utmost for His Highest* (Grand Rapids, MI: Discovery House Publishers, 1992), January 19.

11

Will You Stand with Jesus?

When *The New York Times* asked a handful of horror movie directors, producers and screenwriters to name the films that had scared them when they were younger, top candidates for scariest movies included Bela Lugosi's 1931 classic *Dracula*; films from the 1970s (*The Exorcist* and *The Texas Chainsaw Massacre*); and Stephen King's *The Shining.*

King is the world's leading horror writer thanks to his many books, more than 70 of which have been turned into movies, TV series or short films, like *Carrie*, *Salem's Lot*, *Pet Cemetery*, *Misery*, *The Shawshank Redemption* and *The Green Mile.*

One of my all-time favorite fright films is King's TV miniseries *The Stand*. Like most successful horror writers, King comes up with entertaining new ways to address old concepts, like the problem of good versus evil. As *The Stand* begins, we learn that a devastating plague has wiped out 99.3 percent of the population of the U.S. Those who survived the plague have begun to experience visionary dreams in which they are summoned by both God and the devil and asked to choose who they will follow.

God is represented by Abigail, a 106-year-old African-American woman who welcomes plague survivors to her little farmhouse in Nebraska, where they sing hymns like "What a Friend We Have in Jesus" and hear sermons encouraging them to love God and stand against the devil.

The devil's representative is Randall Flagg, who establishes his headquarters in Las Vegas. Flagg seems like a pretty charismatic guy until he gets angry, and his dark, destructive nature rises to the surface.

The characters in *The Stand* face a clear choice: Will you stand with God or will you stand with the devil? Today, you and I face a similar choice, as Paul explained in his letter to the Ephesians:

> Finally, be strong in the Lord and in the strength of his might. Put on the whole armor of God, that you may be able to stand against the wiles of the devil. For we are not contending against flesh and blood, but against the principalities, against the powers, against the world rulers of this present darkness, against the spiritual hosts of wickedness in the heavenly places. Therefore take the whole armor of God, that you may be able to withstand in the evil day, and having done all, to stand. Stand

> therefore, having girded your loins with truth, and having put on the breastplate of righteousness, and having shod your feet with the equipment of the gospel of peace; besides all these, taking the shield of faith, with which you can quench all the flaming darts of the evil one. And take the helmet of salvation, and the sword of the Spirit, which is the word of God. Pray at all times in the Spirit, with all prayer and supplication (Eph. 6:10-18).

If you're reading this book, you have probably already made your choice to be on God's side. But it's not simple and easy. That's why Paul warns us to be armored and equipped so that we can win the battle of good versus evil being waged in our own souls every day.

If you want to stand with God and be strong in your battle against evil, I believe you will need to commit yourself to doing three things:

1. Standing off
2. Standing out
3. Standing up

The Power of Standing Off

For decades, a group of scientists has been tinkering with human genes to create "bulletproof skin" that can stop bullets and prevent some of the tens of thousands of gun-related deaths that happen around the world every year. Meanwhile, researchers are using a synthetic form of spider silk to create thin bulletproof fabrics that are stronger than the body armor that police and soldiers currently wear.

I wish these scientists well; meanwhile, I will try to avoid situations or places where gun deaths may occur. That's what I mean by standing off.

Dictionaries define a "standoffish" person as someone who is cold, unfriendly or distant. And while you probably don't want to be standoffish toward your family or your neighbors, when it comes to evil, you want to be as standoffish as you can.

In the Bible, we are repeatedly instructed to stand off from evil by pursuing *holiness*, which comes from the Greek word *hagios*, meaning *separate*. As Peter explains, we should separate ourselves from evil and sin so that we can experience God's holiness:

> As obedient children, do not be conformed to the passions of your former ignorance, but as he who called you is holy, be holy yourselves in all your conduct; since it is written, "You shall be holy, for I am holy" (1 Pet. 1:14-16).

Peter and Stephen King make the same point: good and evil are incompatible. You can devote yourself to Abigail in Nebraska, or you can join up with Randall Flagg in Las Vegas; but you can't do both. So which way are you going to go?

I believe that many Christians today have a weak grasp of what holiness means, but if we examine Old Testament passages about the Jewish temple and tabernacle, we can see more clearly what holiness really requires of us.

Located in the center of the Jewish temple was an area called the holy of holies, a place so sacred that the presence of God (the *Shekinah*) could dwell there. Only one person—the high priest—could enter it, and this only once a year: on Yom Kippur, the Day of Atonement. When the high priest entered the holy of holies, he would approach the mercy seat to seek God and plead for atonement for the sins of the people.

Every year when the high priest entered the holy of holies, he did so with fear and trembling. In fact, other priests would tie a rope around the high priest's waist so they could retrieve him if he was struck dead by the glory and majesty of God.

I hope you are getting a clearer picture of what holiness truly means, but that doesn't mean I want you to tie a rope around your waist before you come to church next Sunday! Today, God offers you and me a different way to experience holiness.

Christians have something like the holy of holies, but it's not a sacred space in a building that can only be entered once a year. Instead, you and I are now living, human temples. If you are a follower of Jesus Christ, you can experience God's presence in your life every day, because God's Spirit has come to reside and dwell in you like God formerly dwelled in the holy of holies.

As Paul explains, this presence of God within us requires that we be standoffish toward those things that offend the holiness of God:

> Do you not know that your bodies are members of Christ? Shall I therefore take the members of Christ and make them members of a prostitute? Never! Do you

> not know that he who joins himself to a prostitute becomes one body with her? For, as it is written, "The two shall become one flesh." But he who is united to the Lord becomes one spirit with him. Shun immorality. Every other sin which a man commits is outside the body; but the immoral man sins against his own body. Do you not know that your body is a temple of the Holy Spirit within you, which you have from God? You are not your own; you were bought with a price. So glorify God in your body (1 Cor. 6:15-20).

So what does it mean for you and me to realize that the holy of holies that once caused such fear and trembling for the high priest now resides within us? Instead of a building made of stone and mortar, our bodies are now temples of God's Holy Spirit. That's why God doesn't want us to pollute or desecrate the bodily temple through defilement and sin.

If you want to be on God's side rather than on Satan's, you need to learn to be standoffish toward evil. This doesn't mean you need to be standoffish toward sinful people. We are to love and serve and pray for them. But as we live in this sinful and fallen world, we stand off when it comes to sin. God doesn't want us to be standoffish with respect to people; but with respect to sin, stand off.

Standing Out for God

"GOD HATES FAGS!!!" At least that's what the members of one small Kansas church believe, and they promote their angry message by carrying signs and banners to churches and funerals across the country.

I believe that God wants those of us who follow Him to stand out and be different from other people, but have you ever noticed that some Christians seem to stand out for all the wrong reasons?

Remember the Florida pastor who declared that he would burn a Koran—Islam's book of scriptures—at his church on September 11, 2010, the ninth anniversary of the 9/11 attacks on the World Trade Center and the Pentagon? The pastor was eventually talked out of acting on his silly plan, but not before he gained worldwide media coverage and inspired angry protests and even deaths in the Middle East.

I read two newspapers a day and subscribe to about 30 magazines to keep track of news and developments in the world. Unfortunately, I often read stories about Christians who stand out for all the wrong reasons. The list would include television preachers who abuse money, sex and power; priests who molest precious children; Christian businessmen and women who feature the little fish symbol on their business cards but fail to practice integrity in their work; politicians who say they love God but lace their speeches and campaign literature with hatred and fear; as well as normal, everyday Christians like you and me who don't always practice what we preach.

Once, I had my own experience of standing out for the wrong reasons. After graduating from high school, a buddy and I traveled to Alaska on a freighter ship. We were young and were having a good time, so we neglected to concentrate on the mandatory (and boring) safety briefings. That's why we were so surprised one morning when the freighter's alarms went off. We jumped out of our beds, hastily threw on our life vests, and joined the crew and passengers who were already lined up on the deck. That's when we realized we were standing out. All the other people wore their life vests over their normal clothing. My buddy and me? We were wearing only boxer shorts. You can probably think of examples from your own life when you stood out and suffered the embarrassing consequences.

Wouldn't you feel relieved if Christians stopped standing out for the wrong reasons and started standing out for the good they do? I wish we could all stand out for Jesus in the ways described by the Catholic priest who wrote the popular hymn "They'll Know We Are Christians by Our Love." The hymn echoes the words of Jesus, who told His disciples, "By this all men will know that you are my disciples, if you have love for one another" (John 13:35).

History gives us an example of someone who stood out by embodying Christ's love for humanity. Her name was Clara Barton.

It was 1862, and yet another young man was dying on one of the bloody battlefields of America's Civil War. Horribly injured and convulsed by pain, the soldier knew that he would not survive without help, but he also knew there was no help to be found in this godforsaken deathscape.

As he lay there in pain, he began to think about his wife. In his mind he could see her face so clearly. She was beautiful to him. He remembered her as last he had seen her, with tears on her face as he went off to war. He loved her. He hadn't wanted to go off to war. And the last thing he had said was, "I'll be back soon." He now feared that this statement was a lie. He would never be coming back from this war.

Then he realized someone was touching him gently. In his confusion he assumed it was his wife. But that was crazy! He looked up to see a woman kneeling over him. How could this be? There should be no women anywhere near this horrible battlefield, but here she was, bandaging his wounds and speaking words of encouragement. Soon, two other angels of mercy appeared by his side. They carefully lifted him into the back of a horse-drawn cart.

The soldier passed out after taking one last look at the woman, not knowing that he was merely one of thousands of soldiers who were being cared for and brought back to life by Clara Barton, the "angel of the battlefields," who would become the founder of the American Red Cross.

In the midst of unspeakable pain, suffering and death, Barton stood out for her godly love and her selfless service to those who were wounded in body and spirit. She is remembered as an ambassador for Christ, not an embarrassment to the cause of Christianity.

Who has stood out like Clara Barton in my own lifetime? My short list of Christian heroes include Kay Warren, who has devoted herself to the battle against AIDS; Mother Teresa, who gave her life to serve India's untouchables; Bono, who has used his platform as leader of the world's greatest rock band, U2, to spread God's message; and Martin Luther King Jr., who used

Christian nonviolence to ignite the movement for civil rights. None of these heroes was perfect, but who is? The point is, they have been beacons of God's love to a sometimes dark and despairing world.

Jesus once told a story about someone who stood out for all the right reasons. A man had been robbed and beaten on a busy Jericho road. A priest and a Levite passed by the hurting man and went on their way without stopping. They didn't stand out.

Then a Samaritan came along and helped the injured man. This caring soul stood out. He was the one who cared for his "neighbor" (see Luke 10:29-37). That's how Jesus wants you to stand out for Him today.

If you're a Christian who belongs to Jesus Christ, you've been called to stand out as a person of mercy, compassion, goodness and love. That's how God wants you to stand out.

Standing Up for Jesus

When it comes to sin and evil, we are called to stand off.

When it comes to love, we are called to stand out.

When it comes to the gospel of Jesus Christ, we are called to stand up.

During the last few years, I have been reading about Richard Dawkins, Sam Harris and Christopher Hitchens, a group of writers and thinkers known as the "new atheists." But these new atheists have promoted some very old ideas about the negative impact of religion in the world. One of the claims they make is that religion—and specifically Christianity—has been the cause of much of the wars and killing during the last 20 years.

They have a point: Religion has been a cause of division and even war. But they neglect an even more important point: that Christianity has been the source of much that is good, as people like Clara Barton, Mother Teresa and Martin Luther King Jr. and so many others have shown. And the last time I checked, atheists have not created hospitals for the ill, orphanages for the fatherless or rescue missions for those who are down and out. The false claims of the new atheists make me stand up and proclaim: "No, you are wrong. Christianity is a source of good in the world!"

The Bible is full of stories of men and women who stood up for God. I think of the earliest Christians who suffered persecution and death for their faith. And I think of Shadrach, Meshach and Abed'nego. Their story, which you know if you attended Sunday School as a child, is told in chapter 3 of the book of Daniel.

King Nebuchadnez'zar of Babylon had created a golden image of himself, and he required all his subjects to bow down to the idol. But these three men refused to bow down, even after he cast them into a fiery furnace. They said, "We will not serve your gods or worship the golden image which you have set up" (Dan. 3:18). These three men stood up for God, and God protected and rescued them.

Throughout history, courageous men and women have stood up for Jesus at great cost. Today, Christ wants you to stand up for Him, both in the Christian community and outside the church's walls.

You've been called to stand off, stand out and stand up. Perhaps the classic hymn "Stand Up, Stand Up for Jesus" can be your theme song. This hymn was inspired by nineteenth-century Episcopalian pastor Dudley A. Tyng, whose bold sermons against the evils of slavery led to his being removed from his pastorate.

Stand up, stand up for Jesus, ye soldiers of the cross;
Lift high His royal banner, it must not suffer loss.
From victory unto victory His army shall He lead,
Till every foe is vanquished, and Christ is Lord indeed.

Stand up, stand up for Jesus, the strife will not be long;
This day the noise of battle, the next the victor's song.
To those who vanquish evil a crown of life shall be;
They with the King of Glory shall reign eternally.[1]

Today, brave Christians are standing up around the world as they battle slavery, sex trafficking, torture, poverty, abortion, political corruption and oppression in all its forms. There is much that remains to be done. What about you? Will you stand with Jesus?

Reflection Questions

1. How would you complete this sentence: "Success in life is . . ."?

2. Compare and contrast your idea of success to Paul's view captured in 2 Timothy 4:6-8. What differences and similarities did you find?

3. What do you think it means to live a life of significance?

4. Make a list of defining characteristics of how success is measured according to the standards of this world. Next to that list, also make one that would define success from God's perspective. What insights and conclusions do you gain from comparing the two lists?

5. What practices need to be a part of your life to ensure that you are living a life of significance?

6. What commitments do you need to act on or bolster to help strengthen and sustain your faith in Christ?

7. What are three to five desires or goals you believe God has for you in the remaining years of your life on this earth?

Note

1. George Duffield (1818–1888), "Stand Up, Stand Up for Jesus."

And one more question for your consideration...

12

What Does a Successful Life Look Like?

In 1922, explorer Howard Carter made an amazing find: the long-lost, gold-encrusted tombs of King Tutankhamun, Egyptian pharaoh. Relics from the tombs came to the Denver Art Museum in 2010 for a show called "Tutankhamun: The Golden King and the Great Pharaohs." The show featured everything from a golden funerary mask to a carved stone toilet seat.

It seemed that everybody in Denver was talking about the Tut show, which boasted sold-out tickets and long lines that wrapped around the museum. People were amazed at the beautiful grave decorations, which gave evidence of King Tut's success.

It seems that everyone wants to be successful, but not everyone defines success the same way. One popular definition can be found on T-shirts and bumper stickers: "He who dies with the most toys wins." But you can also see T-shirts that debunk this definition: "He who dies with the most toys still dies."

How do you spell success? Your answer will have a big impact on how you spend your time and treasures. Most people I talk to define success in terms of career advancement. This requires that they focus on getting the necessary education, credentials, training and experience to be successful in their chosen career field and climb the corporate ladder.

Other people look at success the same way the man did in Jesus' parable. They see it in terms of accumulated wealth: whoever has the most money when he dies wins.

Some people define success as loving relationships with family and friends. That's not a bad idea. Others view success as having time for comfort and relaxation, like the men and women we see sitting in beautiful bathtubs in those Viagra commercials.

Most of the time, it seems that we combine aspects of these various factors into our own unique definitions for success that have a certain level of career advancement; some measure of accumulated wealth; a small number of close, loving relationships with family and friends; and of course, time for comfort and relaxation. Put it all together and you have our varied definitions of what it means to be successful in life.

In this chapter, I want to suggest a different definition of success. I propose that we spell success like this: *significance.*

That may sound confusing now, but keep reading and it will become clearer.

1. Counting the Finite Days and the Hours

A century ago, two convicted criminals were scheduled to be executed in the busy electric chair at New York's notorious Sing Sing prison. The two men repeatedly appealed to the authorities to cancel their executions. When these appeals failed, they petitioned the court to be executed according to Standard Time as opposed to Daylight Savings Time. This appeal, which was also denied, would have allowed the two crooks to live one more hour.

It seems that everyone wants more time, but we all receive the same allotment: 24 hours each day (which equals 1,440 minutes, or 86,400 seconds). No matter who you are, all the money in the world won't let you buy one single second more than the next guy.

Each one of us receives 168 hours each week. Where do all these hours go? The average person spends around 50 hours sleeping and around 50 hours working each week. That leaves around 68 hours a week. When you subtract further time for preparing and eating meals, bathing and getting dressed, there's not a whole lot of "free" time left for us to use as we would please.

This brings me to my first lesson of this chapter: time is finite. You don't know how many days you have in life. Depending on your age, this may sound like theory to you. If you are younger, you may feel that the majority of your life is in front of you, so you don't worry much about the passing of the years.

When you are my age, though, the finiteness of time is not theory, but reality. I know that most of my life has already passed, so I want to make even more certain that what I do in the time that remains has significance.

Some of us get more years than others, and some of us fewer, but no matter how many days you have, they are finite. Then you are dead and buried, perhaps like King Tut in a glorious tomb, or perhaps in a simpler, more humble grave.

It's a dust-to-dust and ashes-to-ashes world. Life is short. That's why the psalmist tells us:

> So teach us to number our days that we may get a heart of wisdom (Ps. 90:12).

Do you number your days? We should number them and count them and keep track of them, but not with anxiety or fear. God does not want us to live lives of anxiety, but He does want us to number our days and thank Him for the gift of each and every day. That's how precious the gift of time is. Time belongs to Him, and He's given each of us a certain amount of it.

How do you define success in living if you know your days are numbered and your hours are finite? You can run yourself ragged in a mad dash, trying to cram each day full and extract every ounce of life from every second. Or you can focus on living a life of significance, which will give you a different perspective on how to use the time you have been given. Focusing on significance may change the way you manage your time and alter your priorities on your calendar.

2. Invest in the Infinite

The Italians call it *Duomo di Milano*. Foreigners call it *Milan Cathedral*; but no matter what you call it, this glorious building packs a powerful message.

There are many beautiful European cathedrals that create "sacred space" that seems to transcend time and draw your eyes and hearts upward toward heaven. The Milan Cathedral is both beautiful and sacred, and it also teaches three lessons about time and eternity in the inscriptions over its three main doors.

The inscription above the far left door reads, "All that pleases is but for a moment."

Above the far right door are the words "All that troubles is but for a moment."

The final message is found above the great center door: "Nothing is important save that which is eternal."

I studied up and read all about the Milan cathedral in guidebooks and history books before seeing it for myself. The *Duomo*'s architect perfectly anticipated my second point of this chapter: Since time is finite, we should serve what is infinite. Understanding this point is the beginning of moving toward significance. As we live our lives in this finite world of space and time, we need to somehow be connected to the infinite and to the eternal. This means that we need to find connection with Jesus Christ, who is infinite but entered into the finite through the Incarnation. He is the eternal come into the temporal. He has invaded our time/space continuum. He is God, but He shared our flesh, our humanity. All our significance is tied to Him.

One way we can invest in the infinite is to be less wrapped up in this world and all it holds. In one of the more famous portions of His Sermon on the Mount, Jesus tells us we cannot serve two masters:

> No one can serve two masters; for either he will hate the one and love the other, or he will be devoted to the one and despise the other. You cannot serve God and mammon.
>
> Therefore I tell you, do not be anxious about your life, what you shall eat or what you shall drink, nor about your body, what you shall put on. Is not life more than food, and the body more than clothing? Look at the birds of the air: they neither sow nor reap nor gather into barns, and yet your heavenly Father feeds them. Are you not of more value than they? And which of you by being anxious can add one cubit to his span of life?
>
> And why are you anxious about clothing? Consider the lilies of the field, how they grow; they neither toil nor spin; yet I tell you, even Solomon in all his glory was not arrayed like one of these. But if God so clothes the grass of the field, which today is alive and tomorrow is thrown into the oven, will he not much more clothe you, O men of little faith?
>
> Therefore do not be anxious, saying, "What shall we eat?" or "What shall we drink?" or "What shall we wear?" For the Gentiles seek all these things; and your heavenly Father knows that you need them all. But seek first his kingdom and his righteousness, and all these things shall be yours as well.

> Therefore do not be anxious about tomorrow, for tomorrow will be anxious for itself. Let the day's own trouble be sufficient for the day (Matt. 6:24-34).

Jesus tells His listeners that our anxiety can't add one moment to our finite life span. So what does He tell us to do? Seek first His kingdom and His righteousness. In other words: invest in the infinite rather than spending your life in the anxious quest of finite satisfaction.

The question of how you define success is really a question of what you seek. So let me ask you two variations of the same question: Do you seek first His kingdom and His righteousness? Is your sense of significance wrapped up in His kingdom and His righteousness?

How about you? Do you long for righteousness? This is significance. Jesus said for us to seek His kingdom and His righteousness. Are you seeking His kingdom?

Let Your Life Write Your Epitaph

The night before he was gunned down at the Lorraine Motel in Memphis, Tennessee, Martin Luther King Jr. delivered a powerful speech. The date was April 3, 1968, and King seemed to have a sense of his own approaching death:

> I've looked over. And I've seen the promised land. I may not get there with you. But I want you to know tonight, that we, as a people, will get to the promised land. And I'm happy tonight. I'm not worried about anything. I'm not fearing any man.[1]

King knew there were many people who wanted him dead, so it's surprising to hear him say he fears no man. The apostle Paul also appears to have had a premonition about his death in the closing portions of his second letter to Timothy, his trusted friend and co-laborer:

> For I am already on the point of being sacrificed; the time of my departure has come. I have fought the good fight, I have finished the race, I have kept the faith. Henceforth there is laid up for me the crown of righteousness, which the Lord, the righteous judge, will award to me on that Day, and not only to me but also to all who have loved his appearing (2 Tim. 4:6-8).

Some scholars call this passage "The Triumphant Testimony of the Apostle Paul" because he testifies about his own continuing faithfulness to God. Paul assesses his own success in terms of his faith. My prayer for you is that you define success in similar ways so that you will invest in the infinite, not the temporal things that so quickly pass away.

The three sections of Paul's brief testimony address some key issues, so let's take a closer look.

"I Have Fought the Good Fight"

What is this good fight? What is Paul talking about? The New Testament's word for "good" would normally be *agothos*, which refers to that which is beneficial in its effects, but that is not the word used here. The word Paul uses in this passage is *kalos*. *Kalos* refers to that which is intrinsically good, that which is beautiful, that which is honorable. In other words: the things of God and of heaven.

Elsewhere, Paul tells us what that fight has entailed:

> Five times I have received at the hands of the Jews the forty lashes less one. Three times I have been beaten with rods; once I was stoned. Three times I have been shipwrecked; a night and a day I have been adrift at sea; on frequent journeys, in danger from rivers, danger from robbers, danger from my own people, danger from Gentiles, danger in the city, danger in the wilderness, danger at sea, danger from false brethren; in toil and hardship, through many a sleepless night, in hunger and thirst, often without food, in cold and exposure (2 Cor. 11:24-27).

Here, Paul is describing what it means to fight the good fight. He's counting the cost of bearing witness to God in a world that doesn't always welcome the good news. We must fight the good fight, and it is often a daily struggle, if not a moment-by-moment struggle to fight the good fight.

"I Have Finished the Race"

Next, Paul tells us that if we want significance in life, we must finish the race. In Paul's day, races were a major part of Roman culture. If you visit Rome today, you can see the remains of the Circus Maximus, a huge arena where horses ran. Humans raced as well in the Greek Olympics and other contests. No matter which race it is, it is the person who finishes that becomes eligible to win. Quitters aren't winners.

Sadly, Colorado is home to a number of famous church leaders who have not finished the race. Christians in Colorado have dealt with the shock of the moral failings of Christian leaders like Ted Haggard, who was pastor of New Life Church just north of Colorado Springs, and president of the National Association of Evangelicals. Ted's 2006 fall involved homosexuality and drugs. More recently, newspapers reported that a Denver pastor had also fallen to homosexual passions.

I didn't really know these two leaders that well. I had met them. I had always assumed they were serving Christ. Obviously, there were problems underneath the surface that others didn't know about, and these private problems became public scandal after their fall. I feel for their families, and I feel for the pastors themselves. But even more, I feel for their churches, which were abandoned by their leaders. The sheep were given up by their shepherds. I also feel for the Church Universal and the greater cause of Christ, because Christ gets a black eye whenever we Christians mess up in such big and embarrassing ways.

The good news is that Jesus Christ is filled with mercy and grace. If we truly repent, we can find forgiveness and we can find restoration. That has been the case with Gordon McDonald, who committed adultery in 1987 while serving as pastor of one of the largest churches in New England. He also had been the president of Inter-Varsity Christian Fellowship. He committed adultery and was forced to leave his powerful positions and focus on his life. He repented and went through years of struggle and sanctification. Now he's serving Christ again. In 2011, he was named chancellor of Denver Seminary.

The final chapter hasn't been written about Ted Haggard and the other Colorado pastor. There is still hope for them to finish the race, but the finish won't be as grand as it would have been had they finished the race the first time they were on the track.

"I Have Kept the Faith"

If you've been reading Christian books and magazines and websites the last few years, you know that youth workers are worried. Around the nation, adults who work with young people in church youth groups and in para-church groups like Young Life and Youth for Christ have been reporting a staggering fact. Depending on which studies are cited, somewhere between 40 percent and 70 percent of young people leave church when they leave high school and Sunday School. Many of them never return. These young people have not kept the faith.

Why? According to Kenda Creasy Dean, Associate Professor of Youth, Church, and Culture at Princeton Theological Seminary, the problem may not be with the kids but with the adults who teach them. As Dean explains in her book *Almost Christian: What the Faith of Our Teenagers Is Telling the American Church,* many young people never truly have a robust faith of their own, and when they leave the protective confines of home and youth group, their weak faith ebbs away.

College students often come to me, asking how they can keep the faith now that they have graduated from high school (and from the churches or youth groups they grew up with). They're now at a college or university or an institution of higher learning, and their professors are attacking the Christian faith and the credibility of Holy Scripture. These college students are coming to me saying, "Help us keep our faith. Help us hold on to this. Help us guard it. We don't know what to say."

What about you? Is your faith based on your simple Sunday School lessons you heard years (or decades) ago? Or is your faith alive and vibrant? When doubts and other challenges arise, do you cling to God or do you let go? Do you keep the faith?

It is interesting to see that the word Paul uses for "keep" is *tereo,* which not only means "to keep," in the sense of "to guard" or "to protect," but it also means "to obey" or "to submit to." Paul may have been referring to the sacramentum, or the Roman oath, which was the sacred oath that a Roman soldier took when joining the Roman legions. These soldiers pledged that they would obey the emperor and the empire, even unto death. Or Paul may have been referring to the oaths athletes took before competing in the Greek athletic games. This oath also used this same Greek word, *tereo,* indicating that the athletes would submit to and obey the rules.

What about you? Have you kept the faith? Have you guarded your commitment to Christ? Have you submitted yourself to God and committed to obeying Him, no matter the cost?

Success for Today and Tomorrow

The good news is that if you define success in the right way, you can have a triumphant testimony as deep and as meaningful as Paul's. You can fight the good fight, win the race and keep the faith. If you realize that time is finite and you should invest in the infinite, you will be well on your way.

In the closing chapter of the closing book of the New Testament, Jesus powerfully connects time and eternity: "I am the Alpha and the Omega, the first and the last, the beginning and the end" (Rev. 22:13).

Christ transcends time and space. If we entrust to Him our lives, our careers, our families, our time and everything else we really care about, He will enable us to transcend time and space and achieve eternal significance. That's a recipe for success that brings eternal rewards.

Reflection Questions

1. Which of the 10 questions covered in this book stands out to you the most? Why?

2. What is your main takeaway from this book?

Note

1. Martin Luther King Jr., "I've Been to the Mountaintop," speech delivered April 3, 1968, at the Mason Temple in Memphis, Tennessee. http://www.afscme.org/union/history/mlk/ive-been-to-the-mountaintop-by-dr-martin-luther-king-jr.

13

The Journey (and the Questions) Continue

I hope you will forgive me for asking you some very personal questions in the chapters of this book. I wasn't trying to be rude or invasive. I merely wanted to give you a chance to confront and wrestle with some of the big questions Jesus wants us to address.

I realize that my questioning approach may be counterintuitive. If you survey Christian books, religious broadcasts and even sermons delivered in churches across the country, you will find much more emphasis on answers than questions.

This answer-oriented approach may work well in some situations. For example, in my previous book *Last Things Revealed*, I tried to answer some of the biggest questions people ask about the End Times and the interpretation of the book of Revelation. When there is confusion about what a particular verse of the Bible really means, answers are just what we need.

On the other hand, I am convinced that many of the questions we find in the Bible are not designed to be quickly answered and then just as quickly forgotten. Instead, we should allow God's all-important questions about the goals and directions of our life to continue to challenge us.

Every day, each one of us answers many questions about simple things, like which pair of socks to put on or whether to drink coffee or tea. Our answers to these questions will not make a profound difference in our lives, but the way we respond to the questions Jesus asks us *will* have a profound and lasting impact.

I like the way Frederick Buechner put it in his book *Wishful Thinking*:

> We are much involved, all of us, with questions about things that matter a good deal today but will be forgotten by this time tomorrow—the immediate wheres and whens and hows that face us daily at home and at work—but at the same time we tend to lose track of the questions about things that matter always, life-and-death questions about meaning, purpose, and value. To lose track of such deep questions as these is to risk losing track of who we really are in our own depths and where we are really going. There is perhaps no stronger reason for reading the Bible than that somewhere

> among all those . . . pages there awaits each reader whoever he is the one question which, though for years he may have been pretending not to hear it, is the central question of his own life.[1]

Buechner loves the Bible, but he feels we lessen its power by treating it as an encyclopedia of interesting facts rather than as a complex companion for living a more godly life. "Don't start looking in the Bible for answers it gives," he writes. "Start by listening for the questions it asks."[2]

The 10 key questions I have explored in the chapters of this book are based on the 100-plus questions Jesus asks in the New Testament. I challenge you to keep track of these questions the next time you read through the Gospels so that you can see who Jesus is interrogating, what He is asking and what kinds of responses He gets. If you do this, you will see that many of Jesus' questions aren't easy to answer. They aren't the simple kinds of questions featured on TV game shows. They are questions that shake our foundations and trouble our souls.

Thank you for letting me be your interrogator in this book. I hope my questions weren't too difficult or painful, and I pray that you will continue to wrestle with the important issues we have explored together, as well as the many other questions that confront us in God's Word.

Note

1. Frederick Buechner, *Wishful Thinking* (New York: HarperCollins, 1993).
2. Ibid.

POSTSCRIPT

What Must We Do to Be Saved?

It's clear that Jesus asked some powerful questions. He also answered many important questions, including one that was asked from time to time by people who sought Him out:

> Teacher, what good deed must I do, to have eternal life? (Matt. 19:16).

Similar questions were asked in other portions of the Gospels, including this version from Luke:

> And a ruler asked him, "Good Teacher, what shall I do to inherit eternal life?" (Luke 18:18).

Today, many people are asking a similar question. They may not necessarily use the phrase "eternal life"; instead they may ask questions like these:

- How can I experience meaning and significance in my life?
- What are the most important things in life?
- What happens after we die?

As we come to the close of this book, I want to do something I try to do in nearly every sermon I preach: I want to make sure you have an opportunity to respond to God's loving grace. That's what I want to explore in the rest of this section: the wonderful things that God has done for us, and what we must do to receive these gifts into our lives.

Answering the Big Questions: World Religions 101

Men and women have been asking these big, important questions about life, meaning and the afterlife for thousands and thousands of years. Understandably, their answers to these questions vary widely from person to person, depending on their religious upbringing (if any), whether they live in the U.S. or Saudi Arabia or Israel, and a host of other factors.

I would like to lead you through a brief summary of how these questions are answered in the following three world religious traditions:

- The Eastern faiths of Hinduism and Buddhism;
- Judaism (the tradition into which Jesus was born and from which Christianity arose);
- Islam, which is the faith for more than 1 billion of the world's people.

Maybe it has been awhile since you took a comparative religions class in college. Perhaps you never had such a class.

In either case, here's a brief look at how these three global faith traditions answer the universal question: *What must I do to be saved?*

Hinduism and Buddhism: The Law of Karma

With nearly a billion adherents worldwide, Hinduism is an ancient Indian faith and the world's third largest religion after Christianity and Islam. Buddhism has become more popular in recent years, with nearly half a billion adherents. But the faith is varied (there are Tibetan, Zen and other varieties), complex (Buddha's Eightfold Path to *nirvana* is an intricate system of rules and regulations) and demanding (it can take a lifetime to master its many requirements).

These two religions are different, but I am treating them together because they provide similar answers to the question, What must I do to be saved? In both faiths, salvation comes through samsara, the never-ending cycle of life-death-rebirth, life-death-rebirth.

Karma is perhaps a more familiar concept of these two Eastern faiths. In short, both teach that you are saved by your compliance with the law of karma. You try to increase your good karma and decrease your bad karma through the actions you take and even through the attitudes you have about your actions. It takes many, many (perhaps countless) lifetimes to get rid of the bad karma. The two faiths prescribe different paths and practices.

In Buddhism, you strive to be good by reading the Tripitika, which consists of three "baskets" of instruction. You seek to obey the five precepts (which prohibit killing, stealing, adultery, lying or the use of any addictive or intoxicating substance).

The Buddhist prohibition against killing is applied more broadly than you might expect.

It means you are not to kill the fly on your window or the spider in your basement. That's because of the doctrine of reincarnation. You don't want to take the chance that you are killing a loved one.

In Hinduism, you strive to be good by reading various scriptures, including the Vedas, the Mahabharata, and the Bhagavad Gita. As you read about Krishna and Arjuna, you strive to be faithful by striving for oneness with the One. This reference to the One may be confusing, because unlike the monotheistic faiths that believe in one God (such as Judaism, Christianity and Islam), Hinduism worships countless gods, which represent countless emanations from Brahman.

Individual Hindus worship one or more gods and try to serve and placate these gods through various practices. But the chances for salvation are not good, and Hinduism teaches that there are some 8,400,000 hells where people will be punished in violent and horrific ways. The only hope is to replace your bad karma with better karma, but this may require thousands or even millions of lifetimes, and just as many experiences of the cycle of life, death and rebirth.

In short, the typical Hindu or Buddhist spends a lifetime trying to answer the question about salvation by seeking to overcome the impact of bad karma, but that battle may never be won in this lifetime, or the next, or even the next.

Judaism: The Law of Torah

Most of you are probably more familiar with Judaism than you are with other faiths, in part because the Christian Bible incorporates the Jewish scriptures, and in part because Jesus was born a Jew and frequently taught on Jewish themes. Experts say there are fewer than 15 million Jews worldwide.

Most Jews throughout the history of our world have sought salvation through Torah. Torah is a Hebrew word that means law or instruction. The law of Torah includes the Decalogue (or the Ten Commandments) and the Pentateuch (the first five books of the Old Testament, also known as the books of Moses).

But in a broader sense, Torah incorporates everything taught in the Old Testament, from Genesis to Malachi. Jewish people seeking eternal life try to obey Torah, which includes the moral law, various dietary laws (about what you can eat), ceremonial laws (covering purification, ablutions and various ceremonial washings), and sacrificial law (which prescribes which sacrifices or offerings are appropriate for the various Jewish holidays).

Judaism also relies on the priesthood, and particularly the high priest, who on Yom Kippur went into the holy of holies of the temple. Standing before the tabernacle and offering the blood of animals on the mercy seat, the high priest sought to atone for the sins of the people through the ceremonies and sacrifices spelled out through the law of Torah.

For Jews, the question of what a person must do to be saved is answered by studying and attempting to follow Torah law in all aspects of life.

Islam: Submission to God's Law

"There is no god but God, and Muhammad is the Messenger of God." Those 13 words comprise the shahada (or confession of faith) for every true Muslim (which means "one who submits"). Reciting the shahada is one of the five pillars of Islam. These are binding rules of conduct that each of the world's 1.3 billion Muslims are commanded to obey.

Like Jews and Christians, Muslims accept Abraham and Moses as prophets, but above all they revere the Messenger of Islam, Muhammad the Prophet, who was born in Mecca in AD 570 and died in Medina in AD 632.

In addition to reciting the shahada, Muslims are required to observe these remaining four pillars of the faith:

- Daily prayer toward Mecca at these times: morning, noon, later afternoon, sunset and before bedtime. Muslims must say their prayers while kneeling with their foreheads touching the ground.
- Almsgiving (zakat). Charity was originally a voluntary act to aid the poor and purify one's remaining material possessions. Today, the principle of donating one-fortieth of one's income has become an institutionalized tax in most Muslim countries, averaging 2.5 percent annually.
- Fasting during the month of Ramadan, which is determined by the lunar calendar and commemorates the angel Gabriel delivering the Koran to Muhammad. Between sunrise and sunset, no eating or drinking is permitted.

- The Hajj (pilgrimage to Mecca). Every Muslim must attempt to make this journey once in a lifetime as a deed of merit facilitating his salvation. Once there, he walks seven times around the Kaaba (a cubical building housing a black stone). The Kaaba is said to have been originally built by Ishmael and Abraham on the spot where Adam uttered his first prayers to God.

At the end of life comes the final judgment, which is performed by two angels. The deeds of your life and your success in obeying the five pillars will determine whether you have earned eternal life. Along the way, some Muslims pursue jihad. For some Muslims, jihad is the spiritual quest for righteousness and the conquest of sin. For a minority of more radical Muslims, jihad becomes a militant effort to destroy infidels, the enemies of Islam.

The basic answer of Islam to the question of salvation is this: You must work your way to salvation. Some Muslims seem devout and passionate, while others seem nominal, but all of them are precious to God. They are seeking to find everlasting life through submission and obedience to the law.

Of course, Jesus has a startlingly different answer to the big question of what we must do to be saved. Before we explore the Christian approach, let's make one additional stop on our global tour of the world's major faiths.

From the Nazca to the Nones

The shock came in the 1920s, when pioneering airplane pilots flying over the vast southern plains of Peru discovered huge drawings of birds, animals and geometric designs covering miles and miles of the landscape far below.

What these early air travelers had seen were the now-famous Nazca lines. For centuries, nobody knew they were there. Then, after their discovery, scientists argued about who created these giant geoglyphs and how they did it.

Many theories were offered up. The theory that got the most attention was from UFologists who claimed extraterrestrials had created the massive earth artworks. Today, the consensus among historians, anthropologists and archaeologists is that these geoglyphs were created by the Nazca people as part of their religion.

The Nazca people lived on the plains of Peru from 500 BC to AD 600. Based on the archaeological remains they left us, their civilization thrived for more than 1,000 years. Then, suddenly, they vanished, perhaps becoming a part of another nearby civilization.

Scientists who have studied the Nazca believe that these were religious images created to be seen by the gods, who would look down and be pleased. That was the way the Nazca people answered the question, What must I do to be saved? Some of the larger images are up to 10 miles in length, so the gods wouldn't have had any problem seeing them.

But things didn't work out as planned. Around AD 400 to 500, the Nazca people began to experience earthquakes and famine. Then a very strange thing in the history of religion happened: These people began to reject their religion and began to burn down their own temples. Archaeologists see the proof of this theory at the end of each of the Nazca lines. This is where their temples once stood, but they were all burned to the ground.

Perhaps the Nazca lost faith in gods that failed to save them from destruction and famine. Finally assimilated by other nearby peoples, the Nazca civilization disappeared after its people abandoned their religion.

A similar abandonment of faith is happening today. Proof of this trend is the growth of a group called the Nones (nonreligious people). According to a 2012 report from the Pew Forum on Religion & Public Life, the numbers of people with no religious affiliation is growing rapidly. Here's how Religion News Service explained this development:

> A new report on global religious identity shows that while Christians and Muslims make up the two largest groups, those with no religious affiliation–including atheists and agnostics–are now the third-largest "religious" group in the world.[1]

Today's Nones aren't burning down temples and religious sites. They may not even have any relationship to any organized religion. Although many Nones formerly attended church or other religious events, now they are abandoning religion altogether. Some of them are simply tired of religion. Others are like the Nazca–they have concluded that religion is not really "working" for them.

Some find that their religion is burdensome, and they just can't bear it anymore.

I realize that there are a variety of reasons some people are abandoning religion, or religious affiliation, including the hypocrisy or moral failure of religious leaders, the temptation for some religious groups to seek undue financial wealth or political power, or the fighting and competition between various religious groups.

While reasons like these explain why many people are losing their religion, the vast majority of the world's population continues to adhere to religion in one form or another. Why do so many people believe in God? One powerful reason is very simple to understand: People feel they need help healing and repairing their broken lives.

The Persistent Problem of Sin

Do you believe there are such things as sin and evil in the world? I love asking people this question, because their answer reveals much about their theological ideas and spiritual attitudes. Often, people who believe that sin and evil are real seek out divine assistance for these problems.

For those of us who live in the Denver area, the 1999 killings at Columbine High School and the 2012 movie theater massacre in Aurora provide sobering reminders that not all is right in our world. More recently, the 2013 killings at Sandy Hook Elementary School in Newtown, Connecticut, caused many Americans to consider not only issues of mental health and gun violence but also deeper issues of human brokenness and need.

Not everyone who struggles with brokenness becomes a mass killer. Some attempt to escape their pain through drugs or alcohol. Some try to ignore or suppress their feelings that something is wrong. Some focus on work or play or hobbies to quiet the nagging voices within.

Then there are those people who confront the problem of sin in a straightforward manner.

One of these people was a 22-year-old German lawyer who was trying to figure out what to do with his life. Late one night, in 1505, our hero found himself walking home in a violent storm that filled the heavens with lightning and thunder.

Lost in his own worried thoughts, the young man was startled when a massive bolt of lightning struck a nearby tree limb, causing a violent explosion that set the tree aflame and sent the young man to his knees.

"God, help me," Martin Luther cried out that night, promising God that if he lived he would enter a monastery, become a monk and give his life to ministry. Often, foxhole prayers like this one aren't any more successful than quickly made New Year's Eve resolutions.

But Luther was serious about his sudden vow; and his commitment to God, his insistence on finding answers to the big questions of life, and his aggressive defense of his beliefs led to the Protestant Reformation.

It would be difficult to overstate the impact this one man has had on Western civilization. When Martin Luther nailed his Ninety-Five Theses to the church door of the castle church at Wittenberg, he initiated a series of events that would lead to an unprecedented split in the Western Christian world—the split between the Catholic and Protestant forms of Christianity. Luther also influenced European culture, politics, music and economic thinking. He was an amazing man who had an amazing impact on our world.

As he promised, Luther left the practice of law and entered a monastery, beginning the process of becoming a monk. But something was troubling the young man; he struggled within his own conscience. He had an overpowering awareness of his own sinfulness, and he felt significant guilt about his basic nature. Many people are not this sensitive to the reality of sin in our world, but Luther could see it. He could feel it.

As he struggled to overcome his guilt, Luther's religious superiors prescribed ever-greater levels of religious activity: prayers, prostrations, fasts, nights of sleeplessness and deprivation, and hours spent in confession.

When Luther began to atone for his sins by practicing self-flagellation, his superiors grew worried, sending him to the University at Wittenberg, where they hoped that challenges in the world of scholarship would give him some peace.

Luther threw himself into his studies, becoming a linguistic genius and master of many languages, including Latin, Greek and Hebrew. He received his doctorate in theology and became a professor in Wittenberg School of Theology.

His biggest project was to translate the Latin Bible into German. During the process of this massive work, Luther changed his whole worldview and his understanding of Christianity, all because of one Greek word: *dikaiosune*.

The word showed up in Romans 1:16-17 in the Greek New Testament Luther was using for his German translation. In the *Revised Standard Version* of the Bible, the verse reads as follows:

> For I am not ashamed of the gospel: it is the power of God for salvation to every one who has faith, to the Jew first and also to the Greek. For in it the righteousness of God is revealed through faith for faith; as it is written, "He who through faith is righteous shall live."

In English, the word *dikaiosune* means righteousness. As he studied this passage, Luther had a life-changing epiphany: The righteousness of God is revealed through faith, and it is by faith that the righteous shall live forever, not by their own religious works or fasts or flagellations. Luther suddenly saw that he wasn't saved by his own righteousness or holiness. He could only be saved by the righteousness of God through faith.

This was Luther's brief answer to the question of what we must do to be saved: We are saved by grace through faith in Christ. This was not the understanding of faith that was being taught in the Catholic churches of the day.

Luther initially hoped to reform the Catholic Church, but when he made a stand against false teachings about works-based righteousness and other problems he saw with the Catholic Church, Protestantism was born. It is largely because of Luther that today, five centuries later, Protestant churches around the world stress the importance of faith in Christ for salvation. Today, faith in Christ is seen as the heart of the gospel message.

Now let's explore this concept of being saved by grace and see how it can become the channel through which each one of us experiences forgiveness, freedom and healing for our lives.

An Encounter with Grace

Is God a stern judge or a loving heavenly Father? Is he a remote, impersonal power, or a personal, loving presence? The good news of Christianity is that God loves us, as this well-known passage from the New Testament makes clear:

> For God so loved the world that He gave His only begotten Son, that whoever believes in Him should not perish but have everlasting life. For God did not send His Son into the world to condemn the world, but that the world through Him might be saved (John 3:16-17, *NKJV*).

Have you ever thought about what it means to say that God loves you? Not that He likes you, or tolerates you, or puts up with you until you get everything perfect in life. He loves you now, just as you are.

This concept of God's love is what separates Christianity from the other world religions we reviewed earlier. These religions answer the universal human question about salvation by focusing on law, whether it is the sharia law of Muslims, the law of karma for Hindus and Buddhists, or the law of Torah in Judaism. If you want to achieve salvation in these faiths, you have to earn it. You have to work your way there.

Jesus has a completely different message: We are saved only by grace (which comes from the Greek word *charis*, which means unmerited favor). This grace is a free gift.

Our church, Cherry Hills Community Church, is located on Grace Boulevard. When we were constructing our church in what was then a largely undeveloped area of town, we were given the privilege of naming the street. We could have named the street Bible Boulevard or Christianity Court or Sinner's Street, but we decided to call it Grace Boulevard because of our bedrock belief that we are saved by grace. We have pitched our tent on Grace Boulevard, and we invite everyone to join us.

What is grace? Let me explain with a semi-embarrassing story from my own life. More than 30 years ago, I was driving my car down a local street. When I looked in my rearview mirror, I saw something no one wants to see: the flashing red lights of a police cruiser.

I pulled over on the side of the street, rolled down my window and waited for the officer to approach.

"Do you know why I pulled you over?" he asked.

"I'm sorry, officer," I said, in my most deferential tone. "I don't."

"Well, you failed to stop at the stop sign a few blocks back. You slowed down, but never really stopped."

I had no reason to doubt him.

"I'm going to have to write you a ticket," he said. "Let me see your driver's license."

Suddenly, I knew I might be in worse trouble. I had been living in Colorado for two years, but the license I handed this officer was my California driver's license.

"Are you visiting here?" he asked.

"No," I said, "I live here."

"How long have you lived here?"

"Two years, officer."

Silence ensued as the policeman looked at my license then looked at me.

"You are driving without a valid Colorado license," he said. "I need to write a ticket for both your failure to stop and your lack of a valid license."

"I understand," I said, quickly calculating in my mind what kind of bill I was running up.

I watched as the officer walked back toward his patrol car, and waited as he wrote up the ticket. Then he came back to my window.

"What do you do here in Colorado?"

"I am the pastor of that church right there," I told him.

"Do you mean like a minister and everything?" he asked.

"Yes, sir."

He looked at me again and then suddenly tore up the traffic ticket he had written.

"Listen, if you are a pastor, you've already got enough trouble in your life. Just promise me you will go get a Colorado drivers license tomorrow."

"I will, officer," I told him. "I promise."

That episode was a powerful example of grace. I had violated the law. I had no excuse for not having a valid license. I was clearly in the wrong. But instead of paying the consequences of my violation of the law, I was forgiven and sent on my way.

My encounter with the gracious traffic cop is similar to the sinner's encounter with the loving God. God judges our lives to see if we measure up to His ideal for humanity. Unfortunately, because of our brokenness and sin, we inevitably fail to live up to His holy and perfect standards. But just when it seems that He is ready to punish us for our sins, His grace intervenes. God tears up our traffic ticket and forgives us.

Do you believe this? Do you have faith in the God who forgives?

A Faith that Sustains Us

What is faith? The late Paul E. Little, who wrote several Christian books, including *Know Why You Believe,* once created a definition that seems to fit many people: "Faith is believing in things you know aren't true."

That's the way it is with some people. They say they subscribe to the Christian faith—a faith that teaches that God loves us—but they don't really believe it. Maybe they would like to believe it, but deep inside they don't. As a result, there is a gap between faith and reality.

A much stronger version of faith was on display in the summer of 2012, when a man named Nik Wallenda crossed over Niagara Falls on an 1,800-foot long tightrope. By stepping out onto that tightrope, Wallenda—a member of the famous flying Wallenda family of daredevils and performers—expressed faith in two things: in his ability as a tightrope walker and in the rope that stretched the length of six football fields across the falls that roared 200 feet below.

Wallenda did not simply affirm his faith by making a statement: "I believe my rope can hold me." Instead, he expressed his faith by putting it into action, one step after another over the water.

This wasn't the first time a daredevil successfully crossed Niagara Falls on a rope. That honor is held by the Great Blondin, who walked 1,100 feet over the falls in 1859, as thousands of people looked on from the safety of land. In 1860, the Great Blondin was back again, trying something even more audacious. This time he pushed a wheelbarrow across the wire.

The Prince of Wales happened to be among the audience watching from below during this amazing performance. When the Great Blondin finished this second walk across the falls and was told the Prince had watched the whole thing, he decided to approach the Prince and speak to him.

"Sir, I am about to go across the tightrope again," he said. "Do you think I can do it safely?"

"Of course," said the Prince of Wales.

"Well, do you think I can carry a person across safely?"

The Prince of Wales hesitated a moment before replying, "Well, I think so."

Then the Great Blondin stunned the Prince by asking, "Would you like to be that person?"

"Absolutely not," said the Prince.

Thanks to this story, we are beginning to understand more about faith. Faith is not static. It is dynamic. It requires a decision. It demands action. If you really have faith in God, you don't merely believe, but you put your belief to the test in real life. You say, "Lord, okay. Here I am. I trust You. Carry me. Carry me to that distant shore. Hold onto me and never let me go through all the days of my life." That's what faith looks like.

Years ago, I met Billy Graham, who is one of my heroes. At the time, I was serving on the national board for the Fellowship of Christian Athletes. One of my fellow board members was Billy Graham's daughter, Anne. One weekend during one of our board meetings, Billy Graham showed up. I rushed to meet him and shake his hand. My wife, Barb, hurriedly took a photo. I felt like an enthusiastic teenager meeting a famous movie star or celebrity.

But my love for Billy Graham is more than celebrity worship. I also respect him as a global evangelist. Billy Graham has probably introduced more people to Jesus than any other human being in history.

One of the things I respect most about Graham, who has retired from public work due to age and illness, is that he didn't merely tell people to believe in Jesus. He asked them to put belief into action by taking an actual step of faith.

If you have ever been to any of his crusades, you know exactly what I am talking about. It is the moment that comes in every crusade when he makes the altar call and invites people to get up out of their seats and walk down to the front of the stadium or arena and accept Jesus Christ as their Lord and Savior. Typically, as Graham issues the invitation to come forward, the choir begins singing the hymn "Just as I Am Without One Plea." It is exciting to be at one of these crusades and see hundreds or thousands of people streaming down onto the field.

Couldn't all this be done from the comfort of the seats? Of course. You can accept Jesus sitting down. But Graham knew that faith is more than a concept or a belief. Faith must be active.

You must make a decision. You must step out onto the tightrope and walk one step after another.

How Will You Respond to God's Gracious Invitation?

God loves you and He wants you to experience forgiveness from your brokenness and sins. He is inviting you to love Him back and enter into an eternal relationship with Him. Will you accept His invitation?

I can remember the second I accepted Christ's invitation to me and stepped out in faith. I was five years old, and my mother had been teaching me about God, and she asked me if I wanted to accept Christ as my Savior.

"Yes, I do," I told her.

I made that decision when I knelt by my mother's side. I asked Jesus into my heart and I said a prayer with my mom. I prayed the words that she gave me to pray: "Lord Jesus, come into my heart. Be my Lord and Savior. Forgive me of my sin. Come and be my Lord. I want to live the rest of my life for You."

That was 61 years ago. My journey with Jesus has been a long ride. He has never let go of me. I know there have been times through the years when I have let go of Him, but He has never let go of me. Together, we are bound for the other shore. I made that decision and I am saved by grace through faith.

What about you? Do you believe that God loves you and that He sent His Son, Jesus, to save you from your sins? Do you have faith in God?

If so, are you willing to take a step of faith and trust Him with your life?

This question may be the single most important question I need to ask you out of all the many questions in this book. If you are willing to step out in faith and trust God with your life, then would you pray this simple prayer with me?

Jesus, thank You for dying to save me from my sins. I am a broken, lost soul. I am a sinner in need of grace. I am in need of Your forgiveness and healing. I believe You are the God who created the entire universe, and I believe You can create a new heart within me. Lord, I trust You to do this and am stepping out in faith to receive Your grace.

Forgive me of my sins. Thank You for dying on the cross for me. Wash me whiter than snow. Lord, come and sit on the throne of my life so that You are in charge of what I do. From this day forth I will seek to follow You. Lord, bring me into Your family. Save me by Your grace. Give me eternal life, Lord Jesus. I will trust You and love You. Thank You for Your love. I pray this in Your name. Amen.

Note

1. Kimberly Winston, "The 'Nones' Now Form the World's Third-Largest 'Religion'," Religion News Service, December 18, 2012. http://www.religionnews.com/2012/12/18/unbelief-is-now-the-worlds-third-largest-religion/.